Bluffer's®

GUIDE TO

GOLF

ADAM RUCK

© Haynes Publishing 2018
Published June 2018

All rights reserved. No part of this publication
may be reproduced, stored in a retrieval system
or transmitted in any form or by any means, electronic,
mechanical, photocopying, recording or otherwise,
without the prior permission from Haynes Publishing.

A CIP Catalogue record for this book
is available from the British Library.

ISBN: 978 1 78521 240 6

Library of Congress control no. 2018932883

Published by Haynes Publishing,
Sparkford, Yeovil, Somerset BA22 7JJ
Tel: 01963 440635
Int. tel: +44 1963 440635
Website: www.haynes.com

Printed in Malaysia.

Bluffer's Guide®, Bluffer's® and Bluff Your Way®
are registered trademarks.

Series Editor: David Allsop.
Front cover illustration by Alan Capel.

CONTENTS

─────────── *ß* ───────────

Golfers can be quite difficult, withdrawn and hard to talk to, especially before, during and after an important game – in other words, all the time.

────────────────────

THE NEVER-ENDING PAGEANT

You may think you can hold your own when conversation around the dinner table settles on golf's inexhaustible fascination. Don't get overconfident: golf's greatest exponents don't claim to understand, or have mastered, the game. 'Deceptively simple and endlessly complicated, rewarding and maddening' was Arnold Palmer's definition; at least, we think it was golf he was talking about, not Mrs Palmer. Mark Twain is credited with 'a good walk spoiled', a common reaction after a round that started well but ended in disappointment. Neither is exactly the last word on 'that never-ending pageant, which men call Golf' (PG Wodehouse).

Often dismissed as a pastime for old buffers, golf is in fact the bluffer's game par excellence. At its simplest, it is about pretending to be a better, or a worse, golfer than you are. At a more advanced level, it is about bluffing your way to victory, or at least a less ignominious defeat, in any number of ways that come under the broad umbrella of psychological warfare. Your greatest strength is the extent to which you are successful in reading and playing your opponent, not the ball.

" Golf is deceptively simple and endlessly complicated …. rewarding and maddening … the greatest game mankind has ever invented"
Arnold Palmer

By your words, actions, body language, deployment of the rule book and even your choice of outfit, you can bluff your adversary into using the wrong club, conceding a putt or accepting a penalty. You can inspire in him* thoughts of self-fulfilling defeatism or lift him up to an exalted plane of fatal overconfidence. You may even be able to bluff yourself into playing a better shot. All of these invaluable tricks of the trade will be explained in the pages that follow, along with the

* Gender matters. Golf is a game of few words, or should be. It is in this spirit of economy, and not out of any gender bias, that we have employed the shorter and simpler forms 'he', 'him' and 'man' in preference to the longer 'he and/or she', 'him and/or her' and 'man and/or woman'. As any bluffer will tell you, egalitarianism is alive and well on the golf course. Though not necessarily in the clubhouse…

basic technical and background information about golf and its culture required for the armchair golfer to pass muster in polite society.

Will golf make you a better person? Nothing could be less certain. It may well have the opposite effect, rendering you disappointed, bitter and poorer than you might otherwise have been when you count the cost of membership subscriptions, green fees, Kevlar-reinforced rescue clubs, self-propelling electric trolleys, miracle-fibre breathable waterproofs, lost bets, hefty supplements for air travel, divorces and missed opportunities to earn an honest living. Golfers can be quite difficult, withdrawn and hard to talk to, especially before, during and after an important game – in other words, all the time.

They say golf reveals character like no other sport; 'they' being people who are good at golf and inclined to win. Those who are less good at the game find this so-called truth less convincing, or at least less comfortable. Golf doesn't reveal character so much as the injustice of life, the world, everything really.

But there is an undeniable correspondence between a player's behaviour during a golf match and his real self. Are you a bag half-full sort of golfer, or bag half-empty? Does the sight of your ball in an awkward position that could easily be improved by a discreet nudge of the toecap make you wonder if anyone is watching and think: 'why not?'

In the end, it matters little if golf does or does not reveal character accurately. It is widely believed to do so, and it follows that the better you are perceived to be at golf, the more favourably people will look on you.

Unfortunately, becoming proficient at golf requires an investment of more time and money than most of us can justify, as well as an early start in life, as enjoyed by Tiger Woods, Rory McIlroy and other child prodigies. If you are reading this book, as opposed to having it read to you, it is almost certainly too late to take up the game with any hope of satisfaction.

So you will have to bluff. This short guide sets out to conduct you through the zones encountered in discussions about golf, and to equip you with a vocabulary and evasive technique that will minimise the risk of being rumbled as a bluffer. It will give you a few easy-to-learn hints and methods that might even allow you to be accepted as a golfer of ability and experience. It will also give you the tools to impress legions of marvelling listeners with your knowledge and insight – without anyone discovering that, until you read it, you probably didn't know the difference between a Scargill and a Brazilian.

1744 AND ALL THAT

Golf's origins are shrouded in the mists and mishits of time and need not detain the bluffer long. It is polite to affect a respectful awareness of the history of the game, but too close a preoccupation may mark you out as a nerd.

Nonetheless, you should have a certain basic familiarity with its origins. Golf began in Scotland, and remains a Scottish verb – 'to golf'. It is an essentially Scottish game which should be played in a stiff breeze over nice firm turf – on the cusp between pasture and tundra – at a pace sufficient to keep the blood flowing but without excessive wind chill. One of the game's great drawbacks is the amount of space required per player – many thousands of square feet – compared with bridge (3 sq ft) or squash (just under 700 sq ft). Golf thus requires a sparsely populated region and preferably one with a harsh climate. Scotland – or at least its coastline, the only part of the country with the right type of grass – is ideal. Not many people fancy golf or any other outdoor activity on a typical Scottish summer's day, to say nothing of spring, and this keeps the courses nice and empty, allowing the game to flow.

Irish golfing conditions are similar – not quite so cold, but wetter – and the game took an early hold there too, on the coast once again, the interior being waterlogged. On the testing Lancashire coast, or Fylde, it is often said that if you can't see the Pennines it's raining; and if you can, you should have your eye on the ball. This is another golfing heartland.

Over time, golf mania led to the demand for courses in drier and warmer locations such as Berkshire and the south of France, where Wellington's Scottish brigades put down roots on their way home from the Battle of Salamanca in 1812. Who can blame them?

Whether it was golf, marriage, diplomacy, or some other confrontation that the dashing nineteenth-century Prussian soldier and philosopher Carl von Clausewitz described as 'war by other means', the game has its origins in the perennial conflict now known as the Six Nations Championship. At the time it was called the Hundred Years War.

1421 At the Battle of Baugé, during the drinks interval, the French entertain their Scottish allies at 'chole,' a hockey-like contest played with sticks and balls. The Scots take chole back to Scotland and rename it 'hole.' A new sport is born. One day it will be renamed GOLF, a multi-purpose acronym. Take your pick: Gentlemen Only, Ladies Forbidden; Game of Limitless Frustration; Great Opportunity to Lose Friends, etc.

1457 Golf is banned by King James II because it is too much fun to be allowed in Scotland. Also, it distracts the soldiery from archery. The ban was repeated in the early 1470s and again in 1491, so it was obviously disregarded.

1561 Marie Stuart, a keen golfer, crosses the Channel to become Mary, Queen of Scots, bringing with her several young male escorts or 'cadets', who compete to lift up her skirts and carry her clubs during the game, dispensing gallantries such as 'nice ankle turn, ma'am', 'ne'er up, ne'er in' and 'perchance milady may receive a stroke at this hole'. Soon, all fashionable golfers want their own cadet.

1567 Mary is in trouble for playing golf too soon after the murder of her most recent husband. This is hardly fair. Several hours had elapsed.

1590 Sir Walter Raleigh drops his coat in casual water (a temporary hazard on the course) and invents smoking. Golf becomes even more fun.

1593 John Henrie and Pat Rogie are imprisoned for 'playing of the gowff on the links of Leith every Sabbath the time of the sermonses.' Sunday gowffers seek to avoid detection by carrying the club upside down between shots and pretending it's a walking stick. Hence the term 'Sabbath sticks'.

1603 After a game at Musselburgh, James VI travels south to become James I. Under the terms of the Anglo-

Scottish golfing union, golf will soon be played on Blackheath, and one day as far as Sandwich.

1618 James VI/I grants his subjects the right to play golf on Sundays.

1620 100 puritans, unwilling to remain in a country so licentious and debauched as to permit Sunday golf, set sail for America. Golf spreads like wildfire over there, but not for another eight-or-so generations.

> "…. a game that is played on a five-inch course – the distance between your ears"
>
> *Bobby Jones*

1744 The Gentleman Golfers of Edinburgh organise the first championship and write the first set of *Rules of Golf*. The 13 commandments include 'your tee must be upon the ground' – a rule worth bearing in mind to this day.

1754 The Society of St Andrews Golfers is founded and decides to call its home town the 'Home of Golf'. 80 years later it renames itself the Royal and Ancient Golf Club (R&A) and takes over the government of golf.

1764 St Andrews converts its golf course from 22 holes to 18. David Hume, Adam Smith and other enlightened Scottish thinkers understand that a game of golf can only go for so long: 18 holes is enough for a good start to go disastrously wrong and for a hopeless duffer to fluke a par, and is as much golf as a man wants to play between an optimistic kippers-and-oatmeal breakfast and drowning his sorrows in whisky at lunchtime. 18 holes therefore became the allotted span, and courses have been designed this way ever since. Sometimes they go out and back, at other times back and out, or even round and round. No one cares, as long as they end at the clubhouse.

1800s Golf spreads to all corners of the British Empire. The conquest of Malaya led to the invention of the gutta-percha (gutty) ball which replaced the elegant but expensive and ineffectual 'featherie', which was a leather pouch stuffed with goose or chicken feathers. You will do your bluffing credentials no harm by knowing that gutta-percha is the latex produced from a tree commonly found in Malaysia.

In the early days, the golf ball was smooth. Eventually golfers noticed that as balls became old and battle-scarred, they flew faster and farther. William Taylor added a pockmarked or dimple pattern to the ball at the manufacturing stage in 1905.

Tee technology proceeded apace. Until the late nineteenth century, golfers filled their pockets with sand and, when permitted to tee up the ball, placed it on top of a carefully constructed mound. This took ages, and besides, golfers felt that the quarries (or bunkers) they excavated for teeing sand were large enough and further digging would only make the game more difficult, which ran contrary to the constructive spirit of the tee. Another solution was urgently required.

1889 First portable golf tee is patented by Scottish golfers William Bloxsom and Arthur Douglas.

1891 The R&A achieves the long-overdue standardisation of the golf hole. It would be the size of a section of drainage pipe (diameter 4.25 inches) used as a hole cutter by the greenkeepers of Musselburgh, near Edinburgh, since 1829.

1914-1945 Two world wars had little impact on Europe's best golf courses.

1961 Carter Bros Rug Co of Chattanooga, Tennessee, invents the Cocktail Golf rug 'for golfing executives who practise putting in the office.' This brightens up office life to no end and solves absenteeism at a stroke. Complete with rough, bunkers and a water hazard, the Cocktail Golf rug is a precious bluffing collectable, more highly prized than even the cocktail flagstick.

1962 The Ramble-Seat golf buggy ('for shopping, golf – and fun!') was made for the average-sized American golfer, but needed an extra power pack and trailer before his golf bag, soda fountain and hot dogs could be accommodated.

1971 Research and development begins on the golf ball that won't slice; it uses an asymmetric dimple pattern to ensure a self-correcting flight path. Marketed as the Polara a few years later, it was soon banned (like most things that make golf easier).

Oct 16 2005 Golf gets faster. Pace of play becomes a hot topic. Golf as we know it is threatened by the alarming popularity of Speedgolf.

Christopher Smith shoots 65 in 44 mins 6 seconds in the Chicago Speedgolf Classic at Jackson Park Golf Course.

Aug 25 2017 British Speedgolfer Steve Jeffs completes the 500-yard 1st hole at Tiverton in 1 minute 50.6 seconds, a new world record for a par 5.

2017 Golf gets louder. The Sound Caddy's mission is to MAKE GOLF FUNNER. 'The Sound Caddy is a Bluetooth-enabled speaker that looks like a golf club, fits in your bag and connects to your phone to blast music. Avoid the awkward silences and forced small talk by jamming out to your favourite playlists. Feel free to bust out some mid-round karaoke because fun-first is the new rule.'

2019 Golf gets nicer. New rules come into force. Henceforth, there will be no penalty for breaking the rules, as long as you didn't mean to. 'Players are expected to be honest in all aspects of their play,' declares the R&A. And pigs are observed flying over the Old Course at St Andrews. (*See* 'A New Dispensation', page 73)

GET THE LOOK

There was a time when the golfer could pack with a degree of confidence. For the game, a set of golf clothes. For the clubhouse, a jacket; a shirt with buttons, collar and links-themed cuffs; a school, club, regimental or other tie of subdued colour, non-humorous design and free of propaganda related to sexual orientation, politics or Christmas; a pair of tidy trousers with belt, braces or the full set; and dark socks and leather shoes. Today, shockingly, there are golf clubs where you would be less conspicuous in flip-flops, pyjama bottoms, a Mohican hairstyle and a Black Sabbath T-shirt. And not having shaved for a week. Faced with such uncertainty, the traditional principles of functional golf clothing are worth remembering.

OUTER GARMENTS

The trousers should be loose-fitting to allow complete freedom of movement, with hip swivel and knee snap; and must not get bogged down in the mud when playing out of a knee-deep water hazard. The obvious answer is the 'plus fours', a pair of trousers that end four inches below the knee (hence the name) and known in the USA, inexplicably, as 'knickers'. The sock should meet the trouser and secure it, to exclude any risk of an ugly gap.

"Golf is a sport for white men dressed like black pimps"
Tiger Woods

Above the waist, similar considerations apply, with the need for pockets. The Norfolk jacket has never been bettered. To wear any such uniform today, however, risks branding you a fancy-dress golfer, or a member of a curious antiquarian golf society. That might be a good bluff, but there are quite a few real ones about and you might easily be handed a 'cleek' (*see* Glossary, page 111) and invited to show off your skills, leading to almost certain exposure.

These days almost anything goes. Shorts are widely worn in the summer months. The tie is rarely seen, bared knees proliferate, and the long-sock rule, where it is still enforced in plush suburban locations such as the RAC, has ceased to be a serious attempt to maintain standards and become little more than an excuse for a reprimand.

Embrace freedom! Forget that golfing cliché, the diamond-patterned Pringle sweater. As long as you are not dressed in anything too bright, no one will notice you. But stuff a tie in your pocket, just in case.

SHOES

The same goes for golf shoes. Nothing is as it was. Even spikes have gone soft. The two-tone perforated Gatsby, with matching bag and glove, will identify you as a cheat, a fraud and a hustler of dubious provenance. Prioritise comfort, while bearing in mind that a winter shoe with a summer trouser is not a good look. Spiked rubber ankle boots are available on the Continent and are worth taking to Ireland.

GLOVES

Glove, in fact. The golfer wears only one – in the rear trouser pocket – with one finger protruding defiantly, or two in a V configuration. Left or right pocket, depending on the coded socio-sexual message you are intending to send out.

HATS

Let variety be your watchword. The golf bag is there to be filled, and have hats attached to it. A brightly coloured baseball cap has sponsorship potential and annoyance value, and a long peak to disguise your intentions when you want to sneak a look at your opponent's club selection. The Australian bush hat menacingly worn by Greg Norman has attachments for corks popped during the round. The golfer can never have too many hats. The hatless brim and capless peak come into the category of ladies' wear.

LADIES' WEAR

This is best left to ladies. They have always enjoyed greater latitude than their male counterparts at golf clubs, and that is as it should be, on Tuesday afternoons. Having said that, few male golfers are averse to the juxtaposition of white ankle socks and a well-cut golf skirt. (On a woman, preferably.)

WATERPROOFS

A light set for showers, a medium set for average rainfall, and a heavy-duty set of trawlerman's oilskins for Ireland. Don't expect even these to keep the rain out. Several towels are essential: one for the clubs, another for the hands and face, a third to dry the towels. Some bluffers will not bother with waterproofs, shedding layers as the sky darkens, and declaring blithely, 'In wet weather, less is more.' This strategy may lead to pneumonia.

UMBRELLA

The golfing umbrella is huge, as is necessary to conceal any adjustments you need to make to the position of your ball in the rough. It is made of panels of contrasting primary colours. A plain-coloured or downright colourless umbrella would be much less effective as a decoy or visual distraction, when put up at vital moments and sent bowling down the fairway in a high wind. The umbrella does not count against your allowance (14 clubs), unless you play a shot with it.

> The golfing umbrella is huge, as is necessary to conceal any adjustments you need to make to the position of your ball in the rough.

SUNGLASSES AND SPF STUFF

For extreme weather, a good skin cream and eye protection should be carried. Sunglasses add an element of inscrutability that the bluffer may find tempting. But consider the cautionary tale of David Duval. After winning the 2001 Open Championship, Duval tied up a deal with Oakley and transformed his on-course persona from that of everyday sporting superstar to cold mafia hitman. In two years his ranking slumped to 211th in the world and, still contractually bound to wearing his branded sunglasses at all times, he took a break from golf. Maybe a more understated pair of Primark Metal Mirrored Aviator Sunglasses (RRP £1.00) would have got the job done more effectively. Or it could be that sunglasses just don't help.

ORIENTEERING

The well-prepared golfer will carry some light reading; detailed charts of the course with contours, trig points and water hazard depths; spare scorecards plus a little pad with a clip to put them in; all-weather pencils (HB) evenly distributed around the pockets; and a Gaelic-English dictionary to translate the caddie's instructions. The golf bag (*see* 'Tools of the Trade', page 23) will expand to accommodate a lifetime of pitch-mark repair tools, five-year golfing diaries, Bluffer's Guides and other much-valued Christmas presents.

In years to come, you may find that you have been carrying around in some remote recess of your golf bag half a bottle of whisky, several pairs of decaying gloves, a family of field mice and three sets of car keys.

TOOLS OF THE TRADE

Before you set foot on the first tee (that's the raised section of the golf course in full view of smirking members in the clubhouse bar), you must have a rough idea of the appropriate golfing equipment with which to arm yourself.

The positive bluffing approach is to splash out on the best of everything, the idea being to put a less well-equipped golfer at a psychological disadvantage. This is expensive, requires extra outlay on a caddie, trolley or electric buggy, won't make you play any better, and leaves you with no excuse for bad play. However, it is important for the bluffer to adopt the approach that suits his personality. If you are the sort of person, like Mr Toad, whose interest in a new hobby is directly related to the shopping opportunities it affords, do not hold back.

BAGS

In the early days of the sport, before golfers took the hint from Roman frescoes showing the goddess Diana with a bag of arrows slung over her shoulder, clubs were carried in a bundle under one arm, by a slave or caddie (from the French 'cadet'; *see* '1744 and All That'). These days, caddies are confined to courses whose target market is brokerage golfers, bogus heritage seekers, film stars and Premiership footballers. Even if you like the idea of paying a spotty teenager £50 to insult you, you will need a golf bag of some kind.

The most likely choice will be an enormous faux-leather receptacle with zip pockets all over it, the largest designed to hold the innumerable volumes of the Rules of Golf. A free-standing bag of this kind works well for bluffing in the home, as an umbrella/tennis racket/fishing rod stand prominently sited in the hall. It will also hold any small trees you might want to grow in the conservatory. In years to come, you may find that you have been carrying around in some remote recess of your golf bag half a bottle of whisky, several pairs of decaying gloves, a family of field mice and three sets of car keys.

Gone are the days when golfers bought equipment at the golf club. Only fools, millionaires and those who have left home without their shoes and waterproofs do this, but if the persona you wish to adopt is that of the carefree plutocrat, buying a new set of top-of-the-range Callaways with matching accessories will have the desired effect. Regular golfers go to golf supermarkets in places like Croydon and Myrtle Beach, or do their shopping online.

However, if you join a club, even as a weekday non-playing country member, it is a good idea to have the club professional (universally known as the 'pro') on your side, and to this end you may decide to buy a small bottle of water and a Twix, albeit overpriced, before setting out. This will stand you in good stead and establish you on 'Good morning, George' terms, to impress and put off any guests you may invite in the future.

As well as asking the pro's advice about golf clubs (to buy online later), keen golfers poke around the second-hand section of the pro shop, especially at smart clubs like Sunningdale where members (Connery, Lineker, Henman) trade in their drivers, irons and putters for new ones every other week. 'Apparently (enter celeb name here) found they were too demanding for his game and traded them in for something a little more forgiving.'

CLUBS

Do not make the mistake of using too many clubs. Four will do, but most golfers interpret the 14-club allowance to mean a full set of 14 is essential to play well. This is very far from the truth. All you need is a wood for long shots, a wedge for short shots and bad spots, an iron for in-between shots, and a putter. Anyone armed with such an assortment would probably score well and gain quite a reputation. Tied together with an elastic band, the short set is easily carried, but it takes a good bluffer to carry it off.

The club face comes in different degrees of loft, depending on whether you want a low or high trajectory for your shot. The numbers on clubs are supposed to be a guide to help you decide which to use. As a rule of thumb, multiply the club by three, and if higher than your handicap (*see* 'Handicaps (and Gamesmanship)', page 39), you can use it. Thus, according to this rule, an 18-handicap golfer should not use anything lower than a 6-iron, and only single-figure handicappers should attempt the 3. Try not to get confused between the 6 and the 9.

There are different rules for woods and wedges. For example, many female golfers have such high handicaps that they carry no irons at all, using strange weapons such as the 9-wood for their approach shots to the green. The driver is usually carried for display purposes only ('drive for show'), but can be fun to try when out of contention in a match. Using an iron club for your tee shot at a very long hole is good bluffing. It suggests that this course is insultingly short for a player of your power. 'Accuracy, not power, is the key here,' you will declare loftily, but if you shank (*see* Glossary, page 117) on to the railway you're not going to look too clever.

The novice golfer's usual mistake is to carry too many balls. This is self-fulfilling defeatism, and no bluffer should encumber himself with more than six.

BALLS

The novice golfer's usual mistake is to carry too many balls. This is self-fulfilling defeatism, and no bluffer should encumber himself with more than six. If you spray the ball around, you will find as many as you lose; and if you lose more than six, you might as well call it a day and walk in. Using a beaten-up old ball is not a bad bluff, suggesting that several years have elapsed since you last lost a ball. Using balls 'borrowed' from the vending machine on the practice range is not advised, unless you want to be expelled from the club.

Serious golfers are terribly fussy about the balls they use. Since the size of the golf ball was standardised at 1.68 inches in diameter (in 1990), the important difference is between hard balls, which are cheap and go a long way, and soft ones which cost more and wear out more quickly, but make a nicer noise and allow the artist-golfer to apply spin. Discount stores sell cheap, reconditioned or 'lake' balls, and the pro shop will have a bucket of second-hand balls described, in a fine example of golf-club humour, as 'experienced'. Although they are quite good enough, it will not help your credibility to be seen dipping into the 'experienced' bucket, and besides, having to buy your own lost balls back from the pro is too galling to contemplate.

Beyond the basic distinction between hard and soft, balls are much of a muchness. You do need to know what brand and ball number you are using, however, and declare it loudly on the first tee. If an opponent extends a hand and says 'how do you do; Maxfli 2', the correct response is not 'hello Max', but 'Top-Flite 4' or whatever your ball is. The idea of the ball introduction ritual is to prevent cheating – that is to say, confusion – by switching one's ball. The famous golf sting in *Goldfinger* (*see* 'Golf at the Movies', page 86) was based on this 'mistake'.

The best policy may be to ask the pro which brand the members favour, and follow their example. When in Rome, etc. Most of the balls you find in the rough will be of that brand, and you can play them as your own without fear of censure or exposure.

SHABBY CHIC GEAR – LOW-TECH BLUFFING

This approach may lend itself more readily – certainly more cheaply – to the bluffer's cause. Arrive at the club in slightly distressed gardening or shooting mufti, or threadbare cords and a no-longer white cricket sweater, carrying a light canvas bag with a minimum of clubs, sourced via a house clearance or a notice board in the village shop. Pretend not to take golf too seriously. After all, you are an old-money golfer who grew up with the game and makes do with trusty old blades. As a breezy opening gambit while loosening up beside the first tee, say: 'These huge modern drivers are so easy to use, it takes all the fun out of the game, don't you agree? Are they actually legal, do you know?'

The suggestion that your opponent is cheating may knock him off his intended swing plane, or persuade him to leave the driver in the bag. The Rules section of this guide (*see* 'Rules of Engagement', page 69) may give you supplementary ammunition (using the non-conforming grooves ploy, for instance).

Be aware that some genuine golfers use this approach to great effect. They tend to be the club's young tigers or wise owls who have played golf long enough to discover that a small bag is lighter than a big one. They could be bluffing, of course, in which case you may have met your match.

TROLLEYS

Unless you have adopted the low-tech/old-money/light-bag/short-set bluff, it would be madness to attempt to lift your own bag, and in the absence of a caddie, you will need a trolley. These can be hired relatively cheaply at most golf clubs, but most club members and other regular players prefer their own. And so therefore must you. You might be tempted by a self-propelling electric version, but beware: they come with a handheld remote control that you will never be able to find and a rechargeable battery you will never remember to recharge. The trolley also folds up in such an ingenious way, courtesy of myriad hidden buttons and levers, that you will never be able to open it up again. And since it will be locked to your golf bag, you will either have to carry the whole thing over your shoulder, or hire another trolley when you get to the course. A trolley carried on a trolley does not suggest a high degree of proficiency on the golf course.

RETRIEVAL AIDS

A telescopic fishing rod for retrieving balls from water hazards may count against the duty-free 14-club allowance (consult the local rules on this). If so, you will have to sacrifice one of your putters. More seriously, it marks you down as a cheapskate, as, fatally, does the habit of searching for your tee after the tee shot.

TEES

If you wish to be respected and taken seriously as a golfer of substance, use only wooden tees. The reason they are made of wood is so that they can be left 'as they lie' to accumulate and reinforce the teeing ground in a sustainable way. Plastic tees are undignified and, if used, should be found and retrieved. This can be time-consuming and irksome, especially if you also have to find and retrieve your ball. Note that playing a tee shot without using a tee peg is a good confident bluff, but can easily misfire if your divot (the piece of turf torn up by your club) travels further than your ball.

"Reverse every natural instinct and do the opposite of what you are inclined to do, and you will probably come very close to having a perfect golf swing"

Ben Hogan

TEE TIME

Sooner or later, you may be unable to avoid playing the game. Bluffing becomes more challenging, but is still possible. It is never a bad preliminary bluff to feign injury, limping to the first tee and extending your left hand for the opposite number to shake, with an apologetic mention of your arthritic right wrist, which has never fully recovered from the time you saved your neighbour's dog from drowning. Your opponent may be consumed with pity for your misfortune; or his spirits may soar at the prospect of inevitable victory. Either way, his game will suffer.

THE SWING

The theory behind golf, as any golfer will tell you, is quite simple. Starting with the club head near the ball, slowly bring it back behind your head and swing it down on the same path. Club head hits ball and sends it away straight, true, and singing a happy tune that inspires you to quote the great American golfer Arnold Palmer:

'What other people may find in poetry or art museums, I find in the flight of a good drive.'

A successful outcome merely requires you to make sure that your feet are correctly placed in relation to the ball; your grip neither too strong nor too weak; your arms, wrists, elbows, hips and knees braced, cocked and bent in the prescribed angular manner so as to resemble an irregular tetrahedron rotating and counter-rotating simultaneously on a fixed axis; your body coiling and uncoiling like a wound spring, smoothly yet powerfully with wrist snap but without snatching or jerking the club as it comes to the ball in an even, accelerating arc, and after the strike, continues over your left shoulder in what is called the follow-through or finish. Remain perfectly balanced throughout, with your eye fixed on the ball, head down and unmoving, and your job is done.

A five-year course in pirouettes and pointe work at The Royal Ballet School under the personal supervision of Dame Darcey Bussell may not be enough to achieve this with any guaranteed consistency, but should get you started on the right track. If we were to select a single hurdle, it would be this: the untrained person is not naturally adept at keeping his head still while all the rest of him is in violent movement.

Most of us can manage, at best, one thing at a time. The golf shot requires you to do and not do at least eight things in the space of a second, with several (or more) people watching, all earnestly willing you to make a hash of it, apart from your playing partner who is no less earnest in his desire for you to succeed and has told you twice to watch out for the trees on the right. This is equally off-putting.

There are various ways to tackle the difficulty of perfecting the swing. Try them all, ideally one at a time.

THE NATURAL SWING STRATEGY

Forget everything technical you have been taught about the golf swing. Empty your mind, relax, and play your natural game. Imagine you are splitting a log, swatting a fly, hitting a nail or a computer with a hammer; or performing any other simple task that involves a swing and which you can manage without prior study of an instruction manual. You will hit the ball every time, but may have to dig it out of the ground afterwards.

THE ALTERNATIVE SPORT STRATEGY

If you are having trouble with golf, think of a ball game you are good at, and play that. How about cricket? When the starter calls out your name, dance down the wicket and knock the bowler back over his head for a straight six. If tennis is your game, your tee shot will be a deftly executed half-volley lob from the baseline, flat-footing your opponent who is crowding the net 150 yards away. Sport may not be your thing, of course. Do not let this put you off golf. Many successful players are not remotely athletic. Think of Colin Montgomerie. If you are one of those people who can only relax when tidying the house, imagine the ball is an alien clump of dog hair, or a rejected Brussels sprout, to be expelled from the kitchen with extreme prejudice and a stiff broom.

AUTOBLUFF STRATEGY

Every golfer has two swings: his practice swing, a flowing movement of seamless grace, poise and athletic beauty; and his actual swing, an ugly heave. To put it another way, the golf swing is much easier without the complication of a ball. It is, as the Rules of Golf often say, 'a question of fact' that if there is no ball, the club will not be able to smash into the ground six inches behind it, or sail through the air six inches above it. In order to succeed, you merely have to convince yourself that the ball is an illusion. Any good bluffer should be able to manage this.

The golf swing is much easier without the complication of a ball.

ANGER MANAGEMENT

Golf tries one's patience like no other sport. After a few misses, the most phlegmatic golfer loses his cool, slashes wildly with his club, and the ball, which has stubbornly refused to move hitherto, disappears. Whether it sails through the clubhouse window, over a railway line or into a pond is immaterial. There is a lesson here, and it is all about summoning your latent fury, channelling it and releasing it. You can imagine that you have already missed the ball three times before you address it. Alternatively, think of a typical morning away from the golf course. You have an online banking transfer and a couple of phone calls to make – to cancel your mobile phone contract and change your electricity supplier – before driving round the M25 to check in for a Ryanair flight at Stansted. Angry now?

DRIVING

If the hole is out of range – more than 200 yards away, for most golfers - your shot from the tee will be a drive, which is not to say you should use your driver for it. Of all clubs, the driver is designed to hit the ball farthest, and the farther a ball travels, the more likely it is to find trouble. Most golfers carry a 3-wood and a 5-wood, and these are more user-friendly weapons, and may come in useful later when the ball is nicely teed up in the heavy rough after successful identification. Male golfers should not be caught dead with woods beyond a 5-wood.

IRON PLAY

Every golfer likes to have half a dozen irons in the fire, and at least as many in the bag. The standard panoply is seven: irons 3 to 9, plus a pitching wedge which counts as an iron and a sand wedge which doesn't. Any more irons than that – a number 2 or a gap wedge – and you are showing off.

The iron shot would be straightforward but for the awkward fact that every club is a different length, requiring a different stance and a different swing. No one can explain this, but the best solution is to choose one iron, somewhere in the middle of the range – between 5 and 7, which suggests 6 as a popular choice – and stick to it. Make sure irons 3 and 4 have some soil on them before you set out, and your opponent will imagine you are in the habit of using them. This marks you out as someone who plays a bit.

PUTTING

All you have to do at golf is put the ball in the hole. Putting is the essential golfing skill. Requiring none of the complications of the swing, it sounds simple. But the more you play, the more difficult it is.

Beginners never understand why their elders and betters get so agitated over the simple business of hitting the ball into the hole from close range. Rarely on the green in fewer than six shots, after their travails in the rough, the woods, ponds and bunkers, they feel no pressure. The green is a safe haven, and on reaching it they dispatch the ball with a deft and carefree stroke, and in this way often halve and may even win the hole.

It is the better golfer who gets in a tangle with his putting, adopting and constantly revising strange crouches, contortions and peculiarities of grip, stance and club design. Some grip the putter a foot from its base; others hold it vertical, or screw an extension onto the handle. Right-handed golfers putt left-handed, one-handed, backhanded or with their hands crossed over. All these tactics work brilliantly, until a short putt is missed. Then doubt creeps back in.

The 'yips' or 'twitch' is an awful thing to behold for all but the twitcher's adversary. Back goes the putter head, smoothly enough; but as it returns to the perpendicular, a sudden jerk twists it to one side.

It would be cruel to mention the names of Doug Sanders and Bernhard Langer in connection with crucial tiddlers missed before a TV audience of millions, so we won't. It would also be wrong to mention Leo Diegel (1899–1951), an American professional who missed so often from close range that he devised a stiff-wristed, elbows-out style that became known as 'Diegeling'. 'How they gonna fit him in the box?', Walter Hagen asked at Diegel's funeral.

Bluffers tempted to follow Diegel's example should know that Diegeling was no help on the 72nd hole of The Open Championship at St Andrews in 1933. Faced with a putt for victory and two for a play-off place, Diegel left his first putt virtually on the lip of the hole and missed the final tap-in 'by the widest possible margin' as The Times reported.

Leo Diegel's air putt is only an extreme illustration of what every golfer knows. In the right hands, no putt is too short to miss. So there would be no excuse in golf for that abomination, the conceded putt or 'gimme', were it not an invaluable tactical weapon.

The accomplished bluffer establishes a psychological advantage by conceding putts of extravagant length in the opening stages of an encounter. The idea is to pressurise the opposition into extending reciprocal generosity, and lower their competitive guard. The sting comes at the death, when the opponent picks up his ball from its spot close to the hole and prepares to shake hands, congratulating himself on a narrow win. 'I'm afraid victory may have to be mine,' you say, 'on account of you not having completed the final hole. Such a pity there had to be a loser today, and that it had to be you.'

Golfers do not cheat. They do, however, forget the occasional attempt, or miscount, or accidentally dislodge (never move) their ball.

HANDICAPS
(AND GAMESMANSHIP)

In the outside world, a man reveals where he stands by conveying subtle messages such as 'Eton and Christ Church' or 'Tooting Bec Comprehensive'. Golf is much simpler: the golfer has a number, or proficiency rating, which tells other golfers all they need to know about his game. Typically for golf, the 'handicap' is a complete misnomer. It is not a handicap, but a great asset, in fact the prerequisite of a competitive game.

The handicap enables players of widely differing standards to play a close match (which the better usually wins). The principle is simple enough. If your score is 100 on a course where an expert's score ('par') would be 72, you have played 28 over (par). If over several rounds you consistently score about 28 over, your handicap should be about 28; if your score is about 72, your handicap is about zero or 'scratch'. If a scratch player plays a 10 handicapper, he gives him a 'start' of one shot at 10 of the 18 holes, according to the Stroke Index (*see* Glossary, page 117) marked on the card. So far, so egalitarian.

Perceptive bluffers will have spotted that the handicap represents a dilemma. For the purpose of impressing others, away from the course, a low handicap, indicative of an advanced level of performance, is the one to choose. If you want to win at golf, however, a high handicap is more useful; the higher the better, in fact.

The best way to explain a high handicap may be to allude to expertise achieved earlier in life but for some reason – illness, injury, false imprisonment, a stellar career in business, voluntary service overseas – not maintained. Describe yourself as 'a lapsed eight' who would 'be lucky to play to 18 these days, I'm afraid.' This conveys an impressive combination of past mastery, a busy and high-achieving current lifestyle, and charming self-deprecation – and won't commit you to playing well should your bluff be called.

BANDITRY

Golf is one of those dark corners of the bluffer's world that presents a strong case for perversely pretending to be worse than you are. There are various ways to achieve a high handicap, including deliberately missing short putts during qualifying rounds, and a £20 note stapled to the scorecard before submission to the club secretary. But the bluffer needs to understand that no man is less popular on the golf course than the 'bandit', who wins golf matches by means of his unrealistically high handicap. With this in mind, it may be better to concentrate your tactical effort on making the opposition play badly, rather than recording a low score yourself.

TACTICS

For the man with club in hand, golf is not the most tactical game. Tactics such as aiming to the left if there are trees on the right, or not hitting the ball in the lake by ingeniously selecting a club that won't get you there, are not tactics as Machiavelli understood the term.

The golfer always gives it his best shot, from the first tee to the last green. He does not encourage his opponent to set the pace in the hope that he might run out of steam. A hole won is a hole won, and on balance it is better to win the 1st than the 15th, because the match may be over any time after the 10th. If a tap-in for a 'birdie' (one under par) presents itself at the very beginning of a game, a man does not think: 'I'll save it for later'.

Tactics are for the golfer who is waiting for his opponent to play the ball. For him the tactical scope is much greater.

The British writer Stephen Potter went into this in detail in his seminal instruction book, *The Theory and Practice of Gamesmanship*. Potter is sound on body language, flattery, coughing and clearing the throat, key rattling, coin tossing and jangling, sweet unwrapping, smoking, conversation, apple chewing, insidious suggestions such as 'good luck with that putt', posture and positioning, nature appreciation and deployment of the handkerchief. Study your opponent's routines, and interrupt them. Know his weaknesses and exploit them. Potter draws the line at mentioning tax returns or a man's wife, along the lines of 'lovely surprise to bump into Julia at Fortnum's on Tuesday. You must be delighted that she gets on so well with Henry,' and he is probably right. There are limits.

"On a recent survey, 80 percent of golfers admitted cheating. The other 20 percent lied"

Bruce Lansky

CHEATING

Golfers do not cheat, and bluffers would not dream of suggesting it. Golfers do, however, forget the occasional attempt, or miscount, or accidentally dislodge (never move) their ball, or have the misfortune to trample an awkward shrub lying directly behind their ball, or feel obliged to rescue a tiny insect visible only to themselves and, in so doing, pat down the sand in a bunker. But they do not actually improve their lie, because that would be cheating. A man may be known to be 'a bit sharp', 'bad at maths' and prone to the occasional 'mistake', but he does not cheat and should not be accused of doing so. Duelling is now against the law.

The Great Gatsby is a set text. Jordan Baker, it will

be remembered, won a golf match under a cloud of suspicion. Her accusers mentioned something about an improved lie. Even in the sewer of turpitude and moral bankruptcy that was pre-war Long Island, eyebrows were raised at the suggestion. Then her accusers remembered they had been mistaken.

PRACTICE

Practice will be alien to you. It smacks of trying too hard, which is bad bluffing, and besides, there simply isn't time for it. Gary Player's famously smug remark, 'the more I practise, the luckier I get,' irritates the hell out of every seasoned golfer, and therefore must irritate you. Golf is his job, so of course he practises. All he is saying is: 'I work.' A better claim might be 'the more I practise, the less easy it is to find excuses.'

It can easily be overdone. 'The amount of practice requisite will vary,' to quote Willie Park (*The Game of Golf*, 1896). 'To begin with a round of 18 holes a day will be found quite sufficient; as time goes on this should be increased to a couple of rounds.' That will do nicely, leaving plenty of time for family life and some putting in the office. Notice that Park makes no mention of the practice ground, practice bunker or practice putting green. By practice, he means play.

Two further points may be made.

The practice ground

If you practise something you are good at – methodically, with targets and routines and intelligence – you will get better at it. Diligent professionals do this every day. And if you practise something you are bad at, you will get better at doing it badly. In other words, you will hone your bad habits and get worse. So bluffers should beware the practice ground. It may be depressing, or it may inspire treacherous feelings of confidence which will only be dashed on the first tee or soon afterwards. Either way, it won't help.

The practice swing

We have observed that every golfer has a beautiful practice swing and a ghastly actual swing, the essential difference between the two residing in the inconvenient presence of a ball. So, rather than practising hitting the ball with an ugly heave, practise your beautiful practice shot. If you practise it long and hard enough, you never know, it might just become your swing.

Hear what highly reputed golf instructor Casey Eberting has to say on this subject: 'Practice swings around the house and office are a great form of practice, as is mentally rehearsing the movements you're trying to learn.' What else are the house and the office for?

In contrast to an expensive visit to the driving range, practising your practice shot and mentally rehearsing your movements cost nothing, unless you count the cost of new chandeliers, carpets, children and other items damaged by your practice swings.

THE ART OF COURSE BLUFFING

Wily old Scots say all golf courses are pale imitations of the Old Course at St Andrews, and this is true. In the same malty breath, they say there is nowhere like the Old Course. This is also true. You can say what you like about the Old Course, so long as you don't criticise it. Having, naturally, played it more than once, you will share with friends your inside knowledge: 'as you know, the way to avoid all the trouble is to aim left off the tee'.

Golfers love to go on about how natural the game is. At St Andrews it is. Bunkers grew up where golfers and sheep huddled on a bank scraping away at the grass in an attempt to shelter from the foul weather. More bunkers were formed where balls driven and sliced by bad golfers finished up, their next shots digging up hefty clods of sandy turf which over time created a sandpit. These are called driving bunkers, and at St Andrews they are mostly to be found on the right.

In other parts of the course, slap bang in the middle of the fairway where it would be completely unfair to punish a man for hitting his ball, rabbit warrens collapsed under the tramping of golfers, leaving deep pits from which escape without a ladder is difficult, and the expulsion of a ball with a club almost impossible. These are called 'pot' bunkers, because you can't see them, so it's pot luck whether your ball goes in or stays out. Stroll along with your head in the air whistling 'straight down the middle' and you'd be lucky not to fall in and break an ankle.

At St Andrews this was natural, but everywhere else it is a copy. Luckily, few golf course designers have felt compelled to copy the St Andrews speciality pot bunker. They have also abandoned the inconvenient shared green, which leaves the Old Course golfer scratching his head and wondering if it will ever be safe to play his approach shot, and facing absurd 50-yard putts when he gets there. Bluffers should point out that this is not a criticism. It is real golf, as it should be played.

In imitation of the Old Course, golf courses usually have 18 holes, and they divide neatly into categories, which the bluffer needs to understand.

LINKS

Given a choice, you will always play a links course, because this is where golf grew up – on undulating wasteland among sand dunes. The game is at its most natural here, and played as it should be played, 'along the ground' (bumpy and unpredictable), not 'in the air' (too easy). However far from the sea you are, miss no opportunity to express your preference for links golf, which marks you out as a connoisseur and a patriot – there are virtually no true links courses outside Britain.

The most common explanation of the word 'links' is that it is the ground that links the sea and the land, characterised by dunes and an absence of trees – otherwise known as a beach. Language does not work this way, but bluffers won't make friends by pointing that out.

HEATHLAND

Golf moved away from the sea when property developers worked out that building golf courses with plush clubhouses was a brilliant way to sell overpriced houses to people in areas previously considered unsuitable for habitation. Walton Heath, Sunningdale, Wentworth and Wimbledon grew up like this, and had the New Forest not been bagged for hunting by William the Conqueror, it would have gone the same way. Between the M3 and M4 motorways, mostly in Berkshire and Surrey, is golf's Golden Triangle, with few bunkers but plenty of heathland and an abundance of gorse, bracken and bankers to avoid. Heathland golf is much to be admired, until you get stuck in the heather. When this happens, say: 'I think you'll find that twig marks the boundary of a regenerative eco-biodiversity zone, so I suppose I'd better take a free drop on the fairway.'

PARKLAND

Courses that can't be described as links or heathland are usually dismissed as 'parkland.' Serious golfers don't rate them, with their soporifically slow greens and pathetically shallow bunkers, and regard any golf club with the word 'park' in its name as chronically suburban and a poor substitute for the real thing. The main complications on parkland courses are trees. If your opponent gets stuck behind one, remind him of the evergreen golfing adage – 'trees are 90% air, old chap' – duck, and wait for the sound of ball on wood. If you get stuck behind one, play out sideways. Parkland courses also have lakes. Apart from that, they're a stroll in the park.

DOWNLAND

Golf courses built on hills in the south of England are quite fun to play, with good sea views and long drives possible when there's a brow of a hill 170 yards from the tee and it's downhill from there to the green (or the beach, if you select the wrong brow). Unfortunately, there is usually almost as much upland as downland.

INLAND LINKS

Also known as links-style or oxymoronic courses. This sort of course generally links a lazy farmer with the idea that it will be easier to make money out of golf than farming. It doesn't usually work. Imagine a parkland course without any trees or ponds, and you will get the picture. Put a brave face on an invitation to play an inland links. It's a game of golf, after all, and the farmer should be applauded for not planting hundreds of acres of oilseed rape or a forest of wind turbines.

DESERT COURSES AND MOUNTAIN COURSES

These are easy enough to understand, if not play. They are mostly to be found in deserts and mountains, and to be spoken of disparagingly as 'Mickey Mouse golf'. Mountain courses are usually covered in snow; desert courses in cacti, rattlesnakes, wolves and other predatory wildlife attracted by unaccustomed luxuries such as water, grass and edible, slow-moving golfers. Use a red ball for mountain golf; long trousers and a Colt 45 in the desert.

Use a red ball for mountain golf; long trousers and a Colt 45 in the desert.

GOLF COURSES ABROAD

Golf holidays are mostly an incoming thing. Foreign golfers come to Britain to play links golf, pay their respects and keep the kilt-makers and shopkeepers of St Andrews and Turnberry in business.

However, golf can be played all over the world and offers a useful escape from the family holiday and a welcome distraction from the disadvantages of being away from home. There is also something to be said for playing bad golf courses in good weather in preference to the other way around. Where to do it? This is not a travel guide, but the following might help.

SPAIN AND PORTUGAL

In order to hold your own when the subject of golf holidays comes up in the bar, you may say that courses in the south of Spain and the Algarve are too crowded to be much fun, but since plenty of golfers are locked in to their timeshare deals, check before you say 'Sotty grotty' or 'Val de Yobbo' too loudly in the clubhouse.

FRANCE

Perhaps the best foreign golf nation is France - so easy to get to, and there's no language barrier. Much to the fury of the Académie Française, French golfers show respect where it's due and play golf in English: le green, le birdie, le bunker, le tee, le fairway, le golf.

In the south west, the Duke of Windsor took over from the Duke of Wellington by helping to establish a golf club in Biarritz while taking a break before ascending the throne. He returned after a brief interlude when he found himself with even less to do.

The domestic Frenchman does not really have the patience or common sense to be any good at golf, as Jean van de Velde demonstrated by losing The Open Championship at Carnoustie from a cast-iron winning position in 1999 (*see* 'The Majors', page 98) and laughing about it afterwards.

The cream of French golf plays its game at Chantilly, but there are superb courses all over the place – good value, with some of the best-dressed ladies in world golf and delightful competitions such as an eclectic gastro Stableford Scramble (*see* Glossary, page 117), when a plate of local delicacies and a glass of something crisp and refreshing await as a well-deserved reward for failure at the back of every green. Le Touquet is close enough to Blighty to count as a real links; half close your eyes and Hardelot could pass for the Surrey Heath. Chuck the clubs in the boot and you're there in no time, with no need to pay the rip-off supplements airlines charge for carriage of clubs.

USA

Golf is a more user-friendly game in the USA. Their 'rough' is less rough, their fairways are more fair, their greens more green. Feel good golf is all very well, but the bluffer should not be seduced by it. Remember, golf has its roots in the British game, and enjoyment is hardly the point. A safe bluff likely to win approval at your club is to dismiss the American game as 'target golf,' a crushing term beloved of links snobs. 'All you have to do is hit the thing over a pond to the required distance and the ball will stop' – in contrast to the infinitely more creative Celtic experience whereby your ball will be blown or bounce sideways and will not stop rolling until it finds a resting place in a bunker or ditch.

American golfers are often further disparaged for an occasional tendency to overlook the botched first tee shot under a system originally known as a Mulligan, but now also referred to as an OJ, a Clinton or a Trump. Are American golfers alone in this? Almost certainly not, but it will do you no good to defend them at St Andrews or Sandwich.

It may have been an American who described golf as a good walk spoiled, but many is the American golfer who confounds the sentiment by playing the game at the wheel of an electric golf buggy ('cart'), thereby maintaining a consistent level of play from start to finish without breaking a sweat. It might be leisure, but is it sport?

These hi-tech mobility aids do make it possible to play golf in places like Arizona and New Mexico where temperatures exceed 100°F. Refuse the cart and you might not make it back to the clubhouse, even if the rattlesnakes don't get you.

The more upscale American golf cart comes with an on-board computer that tells you how far to hit the ball, records your score and invites you to place your food and beverage order for the halfway house. The golf may be absurdly easy, but the technology can be terrifying. Distractions are plentiful on the more expensive courses, with regular interruptions to your putting rhythm in the form of smiling girls driving beverage carts.

Might golf be a more amusing game if some, or perhaps all, of these innovations were introduced at Sunningdale and Royal Wimbledon? You might think so, but don't mention it over here.

You should know what line to take on architecture. American golfers are terribly particular about the brand of golf course they play on, and talk endlessly about the finer points of course design. British golfers rarely talk about this aspect of golf, preferring to think of their courses as natural. 'God's the architect here,' you will say, when describing the elemental Scottish course.

Are you a Fazio kind of guy? Trent Jones Senior or Junior? Course design is seriously low-handicap bluffing. If you are unable to avoid the conversation, a good defensive or blocking bluff might be to say courses designed by famous golf champions – Palmer, Ballesteros, Faldo, Alliss, Nicklaus, Norman – are not nearly as good as those made by people you have never heard of (or wouldn't have, were you not such a connoisseur of the minutiae of architectural detailing): Colt, Fowler, Simpson, Dye, MacKenzie, Ross.

RUNNERS-UP

In Thailand, caddies of indeterminate gender do amazing things with golf balls. Golfers love South Africa: great weather, great wine, great value, shame about the crime statistics. Now that oil is worthless, the Middle East has joined the scramble to attract the holiday golfer with luxury hotels and glitzy shopping. Morocco is a fine place for a golf holiday, but be careful before you express this opinion at your club. Morocco? You may be marked down as a maverick freethinker.

"Golf is called golf because all the other four-letter words were taken"

Ray Floyd

PASSING MUSTER AT THE CLUB

Sooner or later you will end up in a golf clubhouse. Be on your guard, because the members will certainly be on theirs. A siege mentality prevails in these places and inmates consider themselves to be guardians of civilised values extinct outside the precincts of their club. The relaxed ambience of a club is a precious and fragile thing, and it is a club secretary's duty to refuse membership to anyone who might not fit in. Bluffing skills are required, whether you are hoping to win acceptance as a member or are simply in need of a quiet drink.

Men of a certain age, who find that the real world has not delivered the succession of pars and birdies they were hoping for, withdraw from it to create an alternative world which runs exactly as the real world would run, in their ideal world. They assume high office, appoint cabinet members, judges, jury and policemen, and exercise power with ruthless attention to detail.

All the things they don't like about the real world – casual dress, mobile phones, fashionable clothing, music, the glottal stop, left-leaning newspapers, the appalling rags young people wear, children, women, jeans, trainers, dogs, bluffers and much, much more – they exclude or ban with notices starting with the words 'Members are kindly requested…'. And if that doesn't work, they pin up another notice stating: 'Members are respectfully reminded…'

The golf club improves on God's work. Nature is a messy and imprecise thing, but at the golf club, all is neat and in its place. One kind of grass for the fairway, a different kind for the rough, yet another kind for the green. Innocent weeds are ruthlessly expunged, wild animals poisoned, electrocuted, whatever it takes. Bunkers are as neatly raked as the rose garden at Kew, and woe betide the man who leaves a footprint in the sand or parks in the wrong space. Members are kindly requested not to wear dirty shoes indoors. Life is not like this, but the golf club is.

JOINING

It is not actually necessary to join a golf club in order to learn golf. You can progress steadily through the ranks – mini-golf, crazy golf, seaside putting course – until you are ready to take lessons on a driving range where the dress code and socio-educational background entry requirements are quite relaxed. However, it is an inescapable fact that most good golf courses belong to a club, and if you want to play golf a reasonable amount – three times a week, say – and keep your costs under control, you probably need to join a club, whether you like its petty rules or not.

There are other reasons for joining a golf club. You might want a social life that you don't have to share with your friends, and you may take seriously your marriage vow: 'for richer for poorer, for better for worse, but not for lunch'. Or you might be in the business of selling insurance policies, or on the lookout for gullible people willing to let you invest their money for them. But the usual reason is to play golf.

You will soon learn to keep your opinions to yourself, your shirt tucked in and your phone on silent.

People say golf clubs are hard to join, but this is not true. As Groucho Marx observed, the problem is not finding a club that will have you, but persuading yourself that such a club could be worth joining. It is a question of choosing the right one. Sunningdale and Rye are said to be quite hard to get into, but there are plenty of less fussy clubs nearby. Be realistic, avoid clubs with 'Royal' in the title, and don't expect too much, too soon. Your first approach may be to join as a country (i.e., absentee) member or a weekday (non-playing) member. That will entitle you to hang around the bar, play a little bridge and billiards, buy a few drinks and refer to 'my club' when out and about doing whatever it is you do in the real world.

You will soon learn to keep your opinions to yourself, your shirt tucked in and your phone on silent. Avoid trumping your partner's ace, and in no time you will be invited to upgrade your membership to playing status. Truth be told, most golf clubs are desperate for new members. But they like to get to know you first.

Don't try to set clubs up in a competitive auction, bidding for your custom. Golf is not ready for the 'what I'm looking for at this moment in time, John, is a deal' culture. You must decide. Choose a club that has its 1st tee and 18th green out of sight of the bar and the pro shop, and you are less likely to be exposed as a hopeless bluffer.

The annual subscription may seem quite reasonable, but there is also the joining fee to consider. This is often disguised as a debenture or a share or an 'investment', but it makes no difference. You put your money in, and you don't take it out. Basically, it's a Ponzi scheme, with golf thrown in. If you don't like it, go somewhere else.

Enter a few competitions and you will get a handicap, and then you're up and running. Ask the pro to fit you in a game. As long as you don't hold up your fellow players, talk too much, make them tramp around the wet grass looking for your ball, try to sell them an insurance policy, or forget to concede any putts inside six feet, they will probably play with you again, same time next week. Welcome to golf, if, indeed, you want to play.

COMPETITION

If you find yourself sharing a round with another golfer or golfers, you will almost certainly be involved in a game of some sort. They will mark you down as a liar if you say, 'I'm just playing for fun,' or 'I don't count my score.' And if you say, 'I'm just practising,' they will direct you towards the practice range with a friendly wave. You must therefore be familiar with the competitive formats as well as knowing how to score and use the correct terminology. Clubs devise so many competitions to keep their members entertained, only the most commonly encountered can be outlined here.

Matchplay (singles)

A plays B. Who wins the most holes, wins. If A wins the first hole he is '1 up', and B is '1 down'; if B then wins the second hole they are 'all square'. If neither wins the hole, or the match, it is 'halved' (although in a competition extra holes may be played to produce a winner). If A is up or down by more holes than are left to play, the match is over. If A is 2 up after 17 holes he wins '2 & 1'; if he is 2 up after 18 holes he wins '2 up'. If he is up by the number of holes remaining – 2 up after 16 holes, say – he is 'dormie'. Scoring at each hole is adjusted for the difference between the two players' handicaps by means of the Stroke Index (*see* 'Handicaps,' on page 39). The score before adjustment is 'gross'; after adjustment, 'net'.

Doubles (but don't use that word)

A and B play C and D. In a four-ball, all four play their own ball. The outcome of the hole is usually decided by the better score, or better ball, from each team. Thus, if A, B and C all complete the hole in four shots, and D takes 9, the hole is halved. To make things more complicated, the handicap difference is usually adjusted in favour of the better players. (Let them explain and try to justify this.) At the bar, let everyone know how much you deplore the four-ball which clogs up the course, just for the sake of maximising the club's green fee income.

Foursome

Two balls are in play, partners playing alternate shots. C plays the first shot at the odd-numbered holes, D at holes 2, 4, 6, etc.; scoring as in singles. At the bar, your view will be that the foursome is golf as it should be played: strategic, sociable and swift. Try to avoid playing it, however: the stress is immeasurable, and not only for couples who have a relationship away from the course to maintain. Typically, your partner is waiting beside the fairway 200 yards away, as etiquette dictates, confidently expecting your driven ball to arrive at his feet and roll on for another 30 yards. It doesn't, because you hit it out of bounds, or failed to make contact. Now it's his turn to play from the tee, and the foursome becomes not so swift and sociable after all. If you are a woman, he will have to play from the ladies' tee, which is almost too much to ask of a man. In the unlikely event that you are the stronger link of the partnership, it's a bad idea to give your partner advice or coaching. (You will, though.) More forgiving variants include the greensome: both partners play the tee shot, then select one of the balls and alternate thereafter.

Strokeplay

Counting every shot and finishing every hole – no gimmes – the lowest score wins. Most professional championships are played this way. In club competition, this format is usually called a Medal. It doesn't happen very often, because most golfers hate it. A strokeplay competition with no adjustment for handicap is called a Scratch Medal or 'The Club Championship'.

Stableford

Strokeplay for duffers. Your score at each hole, after handicap adjustment, is converted into points: one point for a bogey (one over par, net of handicap), two points for a net par, three for a net birdie, etc. The player with the highest number of points wins. This format allows you not to finish a hole, or to make a complete hash of it, and still compete. Stableford competitions are popular with the rank and file, and a rogue high handicapper (or 'bandit') usually wins. In order to keep good players happy, there may be a gross prize for stableford points scored without handicap adjustment. The most important thing to know is that it's bad form to insist on finishing the hole after you have played too many shots to score a point.

Multiple singles

Three is an awkward number in golf. You can count stableford points, or strokes (if you insist); or award points for the winner and runner-up at each hole; or devise any number of two-against-one formats; or, for maximum complication, play simultaneous singles matches - A vs B, B vs C, C vs A; or play a perch game, with scoring as in squash. If you win a hole you are 'on the perch'. If you win a hole when you are on the perch, you score a point. That's all there is to it. Implementing the Stroke Index when more than two players and/or more than one gender are involved is complicated. Let someone else work it out.

Team games

Three or four golfers playing together make a team, each playing his own ball. Scoring procedure varies in this friendly arrangement, usually called Bowmaker. Players encourage and support one another instead of trying to put each other off in the usual way …. until you miss a short putt. Silence greets this misfortune, instead of the usual 'jolly bad luck old chap.' In a Texas Scramble all team members play a tee shot; from the position of the best tee shot, all play a second shot; from the best result, all play a third shot, etc.

In a Shotgun competition, everyone starts and finishes in different places, at the same time. This saves a lot of hanging around, but for some competitors it means a long walk to the most distant part of the course before starting, and back to the clubhouse at the end. You might think there would be a handicap adjustment for this, but there isn't.

Singleton golf

Playing golf alone is not something you should admit to, but it can happen that your opponent doesn't turn up; that should be your excuse, anyway. For a competitive game, try matchplay against the course (par), adjusting your score by the Stroke Index. The course doesn't concede any short putts, and usually wins. Unless you spend

ages searching for the ball, you will play at a brisk pace
.... until you catch up with the game in front. They won't
let you through, or even acknowledge your existence. As
a singleton, you have no rights. You don't exist.

Money games
The confident bluffer may look forward to making golf a
handy new income stream. Before suggesting a Nassau
– a typical golfing bet structure - wait until you are well
established at the club and know your fellow members'
games, reputations and resources. Too soon, and you
will be fleeced and invited back; or expelled.

FITTING IN
One of the best ways to fit in as a bluffer is to make
sure you order the right drink. Sunningdale is famous
for its Bloody Mary, Swinley Forest for a Swinley
Special (secret recipe). At Muirfield, The Honourable
Company of Edinburgh Golfers move seamlessly from
their Belhaven Ale to their single malt at midday. Royal
Wimbledon is the place for a Hill Billy (grapefruit, fizzy
lemon, bitters). You should be familiar if not intimate
with the legendary Pink Jug beloved of the Cambridge
Blues at their home course, Worlington. Champagne,
Benedictine, brandy and Pimm's are the main
ingredients. At The Berkshire, which may have named
its two courses after vodka – the blue is a bit stronger
than the red – the authorised refresher is a Gunner. This
involves ginger beer, ginger ale, lime and Angostura
bitters. Angostura Pimm's is never a bad choice in

summer, but if in doubt, summer or winter, make yours a Kummel. This is the golfer's drink - 'putting mixture.'

You must refer to your club, or any you decide to name-drop in company, by its correct appellation. Sandwich is not Sandwich, which sounds a bit cheap, but St George's, or Royal St George's. At St Andrews the course that matters is not the Old Course, but the Old. It is a good bluff to say: 'Between the two of us, the New is a better test,' although not a better course: that would be heresy.

One or two clubs consider themselves to be smarter than the jumped-up Windsors and prefer to refrain from using their 'Royal' title. Royal West Norfolk is simply Brancaster; Royal North Devon will never be other than Westward Ho!

GOLF AND WORK

It is a half truth semi-universally acknowledged – its seed planted, watered and lovingly nursed by those in full-time employment who would like to play more golf – that belonging to a golf club is good for networking and business. Unpleasant though it is to pull out the rug, it just isn't done to conduct any business on a golf course. You could dip a toe in the water at the bar after the game, but the water has gin and bitters in it, and by the time all the heroics of the encounter have been told and retold, dissected and comprehensively post-mortemed, your important guests will be far too drunk to remember anything they agree to. So don't bother. The best you can hope for is a card with your bank manager's direct number on it. If this means you don't have to speak to someone at a call centre in Glasgow or Bangalore the next time you have a spot of cash-flow trouble, your generosity on the green will not have been wasted.

THE INTERVIEW

Prospective fathers-in-law and employers have been known to use a game of golf as a substitute for an interview. If you are invited to take part in such a match, be careful. The best advice is to let them do the talking and keep your head down (as always). The tricky part is knowing whether to win or lose. It is by no means certain that an older man will want a younger man who has a nasty slice and misses short putts to be his new finance director, or the father of his grandchildren. If he then fails to howl and break his putter over his knee, he may be a bit casual. Golf is a serious business, and there is something not quite right, not quite honest, about those who approach it too light-heartedly. On the other hand … maybe a halved match is the safest outcome.

THE GOLF SOCIETY

Unfortunately, there are people who are unable to join clubs. It might be their politics, family history, or something in their past, best left undisturbed. But even these untouchables may decide they want to play golf, as is their inalienable right. So they form a golf society, and give it a plausible name such as the Chancery Lane Golf Society.

At the core of the society is a real golfer who belongs or used to belong to a club, has or had a handicap, and knows how to talk to a club secretary and bluff his way around a golf course. He acts as the frontman when dealing with the club to arrange the golf society's visit, strides purposefully into the pro shop on arrival, pays all the green fees and blocks the view while the society members scuttle to the first tee concealed beneath their umbrellas.

It can't be much fun being a golf society member, knowing that everyone hates you. The reason for this will become clear as soon as you find yourself playing behind a society. Never mind the numerous infringements of the dress code, they are usually terrible players, most of them without the first clue about the rules or etiquette of golf. They are determined to have fun on their day out and take forever.

"The proper score for a businessman golfer is 90. If he is better than that he is neglecting his business. If he's worse, he's neglecting his golf"

Anon

These invading golf society types dawdle and fail to take the hint when a faster game behind stands menacingly on the tee with hands on hips in the approved manner. Taking their cue from arrogant tournament professionals, they spit on the ground, smoke, chat on their mobile phones, eat bananas between shots and prowl the green for ages before putting, dangling the club between forefinger and thumb as if trying to divine water. After holing the shortest of putts, they indulge in vulgar celebration, with fist clenching and manual-gear-change gestures. Laughter, of all the horrors, echoes among the hallowed dunes – as though golf was about having fun. Instead of vacating the green, they stand around marking their cards and arguing about how many shots they took. Shirt tails out, they swagger back towards the golfers waiting in the game behind, and retrieve their trolleyed bags, which they have left on the wrong side of the green.

If you ring up your pro and request a tee time at 10, he might say 'you can, but there's a society going out at 9.' Now you might question the relevance of this information, but it is highly relevant, because it means when you arrive at the tee for your game, the first two holes will have at least five games of angry members on them, waiting for the last society group to clear the green.

Societies get away with it because clubs need the money, and because real golf societies are often made up of bona fide golfers who like to get together, try different courses and request discounts. They are usually based on professions or trades: pork butchers, taxi drivers, professional hangmen or the like.

Golf Society Man has brought his own laddish vocabulary to the game of golf. Coarse though it is, the good bluffer needs to be conversant with it, so as to be able to contribute to the hilarious repartee. A few of the less extreme examples should be enough to get you started:

Scargill Good strike, bad result.

Salman Rushdie A difficult read.

OJ Simpson Got away with it.

Princess Grace Should have taken a driver.

Lady Di Shouldn't have taken a driver.

Hitler Two shots in a bunker.

Glenn Miller Didn't make it over the water.

Rock Hudson Looked straight but wasn't.

Dennis Wise A difficult five-footer.

Brazilian Shaved the hole.

RULES OF ENGAGEMENT

The *Rules of Golf*, handed down on tablets of stone in 1744, are jealously guarded by the R&A in its Scottish lair at St Andrews, in partnership with its New Jersey subsidiary, the USGA. Over time the 13 commandments have stretched to hundreds of pages as golfers have found ingenious ways to improve their score, each one requiring a new rule to ban it.

Golfers love to spin out the pleasure of a game for a few hours by discussing some arcane ruling technicality, and the bluffer needs to be able to join in. A close knowledge of the small print can also be an invaluable tactical weapon.

To the uninitiated, and many who have played golf since childhood, the rules may seem impenetrably complex and verbose, with much recourse to words like 'deem' and dubious assertions beginning with: 'It is a question of fact whether...'

APPLICATION

It is a question of fact, however, that the rules are quite logical and consistent, being based on the time-honoured

Scottish legal principle of even-handed meanness which, once understood, makes it possible to guess what the ruling will be for any situation that may arise in a golf match, from coming to rest in a rabbit hole to being blown off the tee; your ball, that is, not you.

The Rule of Golf (singular) can be summarised as follows. The answer to any question starting with 'Am I allowed to…' is 'No.' If you want to do something that common sense, human rights and fair play suggest is entirely reasonable, you almost certainly can't. And the answer to any objection that begins with 'It seems grossly unfair that…' is 'Welcome to golf'.

INTERPRETATION

The rules may not be an easy read, but it is a question of fact that they are easier to learn than golf. Mugging up is a comparatively simple way for the bluffer to establish an advantage over a less diligent, if superficially more skilled, opponent. If he drops his ball when he should place it, or signs his card on the wrong dotted line, you may be able to claim a hole or even the match. If this is not possible or appropriate – when playing your bank manager or future father-in-law, for example, victory would be a disaster – you can still advance your cause by pointing out an infringement and generously agreeing to overlook it.

Non-conforming (rules-speak for illegal) equipment is a rich seam. 'Is that a Ping lob wedge you've got in your bag? How clever to have got hold of one before the R&A noticed its converging grooves. Mind? Of course I don't mind, if you feel you need that kind of help…'

Burrowing animals play an important part in many golf disputes, and before striding out to the first tee it is advisable to rehearse the complete list of animals that do and don't burrow, bearing in mind that worms ('and the like') don't. Gophers and salamanders, on the other hand, are deemed to burrow. Applying this knowledge when a ball lands in a hole is a different matter entirely. In order to be certain that the hole has been made by a salamander (award yourself a free drop), and not a worm or the like (no relief granted), you may need to carry a work of reference or a set of encyclopedias.

Familiarity with the complete works of Sir David Attenborough is not required to know that a rabbit is a burrowing animal, and this knowledge is invaluable at St Andrews, where the infamous pot bunkers (*see* 'Course Bluffing', p46) are deemed to have been caused by the collapse of underground rabbit warrens. If you are unlucky enough to land in one, claim a free drop on the fairway - not nearer the hole - citing Rule 25-1 ('Abnormal Ground Conditions'). It may be tougher to persuade your opponent that a stream or lake originated in burrowing activity, but a good bluffer might carry it off.

STROKE AND DISTANCE

Perhaps the most important rule in golf is this: in any situation, however bad, you can always replay your shot. That's the good news. The bad news is that you must count two extra strokes. The fateful words are these: stroke and distance. Bluffers will hear these words a lot.

RULINGS

Case Study A: Slow play

A pair of dawdlers makes no attempt to let you through, studiously avoiding eye contact and accelerating only as required to keep out of earshot. Eventually you lose your cool completely, play a shot to hurry them along and, as bad luck would have it, one of the blithering idiots gets in the way of your best shot of the day, lies down on the ground and shows not the slightest inclination to move. How to proceed?

Ruling

The rules are quite clear about this. You can either replay the shot and try to despatch another old fool, or play the ball as it lies. (No penalty, but don't discount the possibility of a civil action.) If you are unable to get a clean shot at your ball because it's lying in a pool of blood, proceed as per 'casual water' (rules-speak for a puddle). Cleaning your ball is permitted. If tempted to call for help, bear in mind that the use of mobile phones is forbidden at all times. The rules are there to be observed.

Case Study B: Interference

Your ball hits the electric fence protecting the green and rebounds into the hole. Your opponent invites you to replay the shot without penalty. You would prefer not to. The local rules on the scorecard are illegible – you have left your glasses behind. Your opponent offers to read them for you. You don't trust him.

Ruling

This is a tough one. Two solutions. A) Buy a spare pair of specs for your golf bag. B) Find someone else to play golf with.

A NEW DISPENSATION?

The steady evolution of the Rules in response to golfers' incessant complaints took a worrying turn in 2017, when the R&A/USGA announced a fundamental revision. This was born of a disquiet about golf being out of step with the modern world and unappealing to young people, who are said to be put off by the fact that the game is difficult, slow and requires them to wear a shirt with a collar. Many golfers might point out that these qualities – golf's inexhaustible challenge, the pleasure of an unhurried cheroot between shots, and the absence of noisy hordes of scruffy and disrespectful teenagers - are precisely what they like about the game. They might add that old age, not youth, is the growth sector of the market that the R&A ought to nurture.

That has not deflected the R&A/USGA diarchy from its determination to dumb down not only the language of the Rules, but the game itself, transforming it from a character-building simulation of life's random dispensation of slings and arrows to a friendly feel-good experience where forgiveness is key. A few examples of the proposed new rules will give the idea.

'If the player was not aware of a potential breach of the Rules, the player will be deemed not to have breached the Rules.' How kind. Now try this: 'No penalty for accidentally moving your ball while searching for it or for moving loose impediments in a bunker or for touching the sand with a hand or club.' Did someone mention a cheats' charter?

If required to comment further, the bluffer may observe that simplifying the rules governing complicated situations is asking for trouble; and question whether renaming the 'water hazard' the 'penalty area' will really have the desired effect of provoking a mass migration from football terrace to putting green.

Nor can it be certain that producing the new rules in a series of youth-friendly videos that can be watched on mobile phones will be much help, since most golf clubs ban the devices. The keen young golfer with his Rules of Golf app will thus be in breach of the rules before he plays a shot.

To sum up, the bluffer will cite the breathtaking naivety of the principle underlying the new rules - 'Players are expected to be honest in all aspects of their play' - and rest his case. Imagine the Tour de France, or any football match, refereed on the basis of a presumption of honesty ….

COURSE ETIQUETTE

If it is important to know, respect and observe the Rules of Golf, etiquette is a different matter altogether. Rules are about things you must (or, more often, must not) do; etiquette deals with things you should not do, but there is no penalty for doing them. Indeed, the rewards of doing them can be huge, for the simple reason that they will distract and infuriate your opponent, which is the whole point (*see* 'Tactics', page 41).

For example: 'No one should move, talk, stand close to or directly behind the ball or the hole when the player is addressing the ball or making a stroke.' Try it.

If you do try it, the player is within his rights to ask you not to, and naturally you'll agree, with profuse apologies that will not let up, annoyingly, until your victory is complete.

Having stopped standing directly behind the ball or hole, you are perfectly at liberty to cough, sneeze, light a cigar and send dense clouds of smoke before the player's eyes, or sing an aria (none of these things being forbidden). Many a golfer waiting for his turn to play sighs deeply, without penalty or censure.

Here are some other points of etiquette to read, learn and exploit:

Speed of play
'Players should play at a good pace.' Self-explanatory. If your opponent is quick, slow down. If he is slow, report him to the club secretary immediately.

Holing out
'Players should remain on or close to the putting green until other players in the group have holed out.' Moving off with screams of jubilant celebration before the opponent has putted is frightfully inconsiderate. Any Ryder Cup match will show you exactly how to do this.

Casting shadows
'Players should not cast a shadow over another player's line of putt.' Who would have thought of this ingenious ploy, had the code of etiquette not mentioned it?

Accomplished 'shadow-casters' achieve excellent results by holding the flagstick aloft in such a way that the shadow of the flag itself, fluttering in the breeze, flickers over the line of putt, or even over the opponent's face. A voluminous handkerchief may also be used, with well-timed trumpeting. A small mirror ('ball marker') clipped to your belt on a sunny day can also be quite devastating. This really needs to be explained with a diagram and a protractor, but you will soon get the hang of it.

Conversation
Conversation is a key aspect of etiquette: it is frowned upon, and when brought into play in a timely manner can be quite deadly. Silence is equally effective, when your opponent, faced with an awkward short putt, looks at you with an eyebrow raised in the shape of a question mark.

Oscillation
Oscillation will be sure to raise its trembling head sooner or later. The important thing to remember here is that an oscillating ball, in contrast to a ball that moves, is entirely innocent; no penalty can be applied to it. So if your opponent accuses your caddie of moving during his backswing, the riposte might be: 'Are you sure? I could have sworn he oscillated.'

Flattery
Surprisingly, the rules have nothing to say about the most effective form of gamesmanship, which is so obvious it hardly needs mentioning. Say 'I must say

you're driving awfully well today,' or 'That putter of yours is red hot,' and wait for the results. 'I'm terribly sorry, I'm not giving you much of a game,' can be equally off-putting, when you are one down after eight holes.

Schadenfreude

Bluffers should always conceal their delight when their opponent scuffs, slashes or slices at vital moments in the game. What to say/do? Sometimes nothing at all apart from an understanding sucking of teeth and a shake of the head (both useful ways of stifling a yelp of joy).

"Isn't it fun to go out on the course and lie in the sun?"

Bob Hope

HUMOUR, MARRIAGE AND ADDICTION

GOLF JOKES

Astonishingly in a game where self-doubt, morbid introspection and obsessive compulsive behaviour are endemic, golfers occasionally find time to relax and share a laugh. They would certainly not admit to any shortcomings in the sense of humour department. On the contrary, they are forever reminding one another of their favourite golf jokes. Bluffers should arm themselves with a few for the sake of conforming, but shouldn't try anything too original.

One of the best-loved golfing jokes, attributed to Mexican-American player Lee Trevino, who lifted humour to the realm of tactics and arguably won many championships that way, has the golfer holding a club above his head during a thunderstorm and declaring: 'Even God can't hit a 1-iron'.

DOS AND DON'TS OF GOLF HUMOUR

Avoid puns (and birthday cards) based on the ambiguity of golfing terms such as wood, balls, birdie, hole-in-one, etc. These mark you out immediately as a non-golfer. You might just get away with the frogs leaping out of the lake and on to the green at the sight of an approaching golfer. That's right: next to the flag is the safest place to stand. And so on…

Most other golf jokes focus on the golfer's warped world view, otherwise known as dedication to 'the game'. A matter of life and death? Golf is much more than that.

Example 1
Golf Pro 'Keep a firm grip on the club, fingers overlapping and pointing down. Keep your head still and your eye on the ball. Now hit it smoothly…'

Golfer hits the ball which flies over the fence and into an adjoining road where it hits a motorcyclist on the head. The motorcyclist swerves towards a car and ends up in the ditch. The car swerves to avoid him and heads towards an oncoming bus which veers to the other side of the road and turns over. A lorry coming the other way runs into the back of the car and pushes it through the fence.

Golfer (distressed) 'What shall I do?'

Golf Pro 'Keep your right elbow closer to your side as you come through.'

Example 2 (permissible crudity)

If you find yourself in more ribald and juvenile company than usual, you may be permitted to resort to the following, but no more:

A male golfer staggers into hospital with a concussion, multiple bruises, two black eyes and a 5-iron wrapped tightly around his throat.

Doctor: 'What happened?'

Golfer: 'I was playing golf with the wife when we both sliced our balls into a field of cows. I found one stuck in a cow's fanny and yelled to the wife: 'This one looks like yours...' Don't remember much after that.'

HUMOROUS GOLF WRITING

The supreme chronicler of the gentle absurdity and sweet torture of golf was PG Wodehouse who published his first golf stories in *The Clicking of Cuthbert* in 1916, and welcomed anyone wishing to contact him to 'address all correspondence to: PG Wodehouse, c/o the 6th bunker, The Addington Golf Club, Croydon, Surrey'. Clothes and equipment have changed since 1916, but Wodehouse's characters live on at every golf club in the land.

'I have sometimes wondered if we of the canaille don't get more pleasure out of it than the top-notchers,' he wrote in the preface to his *Golf Omnibus* in 1973, and this is one of the keys to his understanding of golf. In Wodehouse's world, as in ours, the keenest and most dedicated golfers are the worst players.

GOLF AND MARRIAGE

These two important concepts are probably best kept separate. No man has yet devised a satisfactory format for a competitive golf game with a woman (and vice versa); mixed foursomes are dangerous on every level, and golf clubs are not yet ready for civil partnerships, still less same-sex marriages.

Everyone needs a hobby, but your partner may not agree that golf is as suitable a hobby as wallpapering or the putting up of shelves. Every couple must find their own solution to this difficult situation, but over time you may find that golf, or at least membership of a golf club (which is not to be confused with playing the game) improves your quality of life to no end. You will spend less time with your family, more with new companions in licensed premises open all hours with billiards, bridge, good if basic food, and poker. This can be a vital aid to the prosecution of a successful and harmonious marriage; and the prolongation of a more typical alliance.

GOLF AND ADDICTION

Golf is a dangerous game, and even the confirmed bluffer needs to be aware that an intelligent interest in golf can easily spiral out of control. Enthusiasm usually leads to hopeless addiction. Witness the proliferation of embossed leather tee pouches, yardage-calculating gizmos, ball-finding sunglasses and other useless gadgets that appear in the shops before Christmas, along with small books of golfing 'humour.'

Bluffers should recognise the signs of addiction. You play golf alone, with a head torch for the last round of the day. You buy a new driver every few months and change your putting grip, stance and putter more frequently than that. While others relax in front of the TV, you stand hunched over the hearth rug making a pendulum motion with your shoulders and downstretched arms without – and this is the key symptom – being aware that you are doing it. Wherever you are – in a department store, a cathedral or an office – you find yourself gauging distances and visualising approach shots. Would it be a lofted 9-iron or a crafty bump-and-run to keep the ball under the branches of the ladies' lingerie rail? When booking a hotel room, you make enquiries about the speed of the carpet and request the right-handed room configuration that will give you enough space to chip happily onto the bed for an hour before turning in.

No one has laid bare the phases of addiction with such raw accuracy, or painted a more vivid picture of golf in the home environment than the American writer Richard Armour, in his autobiography, *Golf Is A Four-Letter Word: The Intimate Confessions of a Hooked Slicer*.

In order to save his marriage, Armour resolves to give up the game and joins Golfers Anonymous…'where golfers helped one another to go straight (something I had tried for years to do, but there was always that slice).'

When GA does not work, he turns to a psychiatrist. 'Even I could see now, with my head always down, that I was a sick man. "Whom shall I go to?" I asked one morning while shaving. I had assumed an open stance and was seeing how few strokes I could take to get around from one sideburn to another.'

That golf is a metaphor for life is self-evident. Its unfairness, cruel unpredictability and inevitable disappointments issue a unique challenge to the buoyancy of the human spirit. It is when you realise that life is no more than a metaphor for golf that you have a problem. You have ceased to be a bluffer and become a golfer. It could be time to seek help.

GOLF IN THE MOVIES

Golf on the big screen is a popular topic at the 19th hole (clubhouse bar). The Bluffer's kcy cultural references should include *Caddyshack* (1980) a screwball country club comedy featuring characters every golfer will recognise. Chevy Chase plays the rich kid whose Zen swing thoughts include 'let things happen, and be the ball'; Bill Murray the greenkeeper with twin obsessions - exterminating wildlife and fantasising about women golfers ('Bark like a dog for me! I will teach you the meaning of the word respect!'). Other stereotypes include the crass nouveau riche all-the-gear-no-idea loudmouth memorably depicted by comedian Rodney Dangerfield ('Hey, orange balls! I'll have a box of those and give me a box of those naked-lady tees'); and the officious stickler for the rules, who cheats. Caddyshack is said to be Tiger Woods's favourite film.

In the 1996 romcom *Tin Cup*, Kevin Costner and Don Johnson are golf professionals Roy McAvoy and Dave Simms, rivals on the course and for the affections of Rene Russo. Costner's McAvoy is the flawed tragic hero, undone by his temperamental inability to play safe - or, as golfers say, lay up.

McAvoy's lyrical description of the golf swing - for the benefit of his shapely student - may be too much to recite in full, with its 'nod to the Gods' at the top of the backswing and 'a tuning fork that goes off in your heart and your balls' on contact; but the bluffer should be familiar with the film's climactic scene when McAvoy and Simms face a long shot over a lake at the last hole in the US Open. Simms lays up, happy to settle for the runner-up's pay check.

McAvoy: 'Fifteen years on the tour and you're still a f****n' pussy.' *Simms*: 'Thirteen years on the driving range and you still think this game is about your testosterone count.'

McAvoy goes for broke and hits five balls into the water, but holes out for a glorious 12, to lose the championship and win the girl.

Another useful talking point is Michael Murphy's best-selling bildungsroman *Golf in the Kingdom* (1971), the story of a young man's encounter with a Scottish golfing mystic. After golf enthusiast Clint Eastwood gave up the project, Murphy produced the film version himself. Shot at a links resort in Oregon, it often finds a place on lists of the worst movies ever made.

For an introduction to the full richness of the matchplay experience, the bluffer has much to learn from the encounter that sees Bond (Sean Connery) outbluff Goldfinger (Gert Fröbe) in a high-stakes game. Gain credibility by referring to Fleming's superior original version of the match, which runs to

35 pages and includes the trivia nugget that 'Goldfinger putted in the new fashion, between his legs with a mallet putter.' Although croquet-style putting was not banned until 1968, the film (1964) has Goldfinger adopt a conventional side-on putting stance.

Goldfinger gives a masterclass in gamesmanship - rattling coins, casting shadows and dropping a club when 007 is in mid-swing. He also cheats, most creatively, by jumping up and down beside his ball in a bunker on the pretext of checking the location of the flag. When his caddie drops a replacement ball for Goldfinger to 'find' in the rough, Bond feels justified in cheating back, by persuading his caddic to switch Goldfinger's ball in preparation for the sting on the last green. By playing the wrong ball, Goldfinger forfeits hole and match.

The story is no less instructive on technique – Fleming includes a useful lesson in the difference between 'splashing' and 'blasting' out of a bunker - and attire. 'Goldfinger had made an attempt to look smart at golf, and that is the only way of dressing that is incongruous on a links.' An outfit of 'assertive blatancy' includes a buttoned golfer's cap, 'almost orange' shoes and plus fours pressed down the sides. Bond, by contrast, opts for shabby chic: a battered pair of nailed shoes and a faded black windcheater. In preparation for a breezy links game at Sandwich, 007 leaves his head bare, not covered by the downmarket trilby Connery has to wear in the film to go with his panther-logo'd Slazenger golf jersey.

But the film version of the game is played on a brassy parkland course owned by Goldfinger – many of whose traits may bring Donald Trump to mind - not a classic links. In this suburban context, the Slazenger and trilby look is not so misplaced after all.

CELEBRITY GOLF

Where Bob Hope and Bing Crosby led, Jack Nicholson and Michael Douglas have followed, with numberless athletes, actors, cricketers, footballers, rock stars and royals in pursuit. From Justin Timberlake to Franz Klammer and the Duke of York, they bear out the old adage: 'it is a truth universally acknowledged, that a single man in possession of a good fortune must be in want of golf.' To put it another way, there's nothing quite like golf for giving meaning to an empty life - ask Bob Dylan. Leading ladies also play: Cameron Diaz, Jessica Alba, Nicole Kidman .... you could go on.

The B-list golfing celeb is a gun for hire, happy to swing, smile and add lustre to a corporate golf day for a modest fee. A-listers indulge their habit in exclusive private clubs away from public scrutiny. They emerge every autumn to play with the world's best golfers in the Dunhill Links event at St Andrews, allowing the public to consider important questions like Hugh Grant's wrist action and enjoy the sweet taste of schadenfreude when unpopular celebs get into trouble for falsifying their handicap. Participation in this supremely validating mutual admiration schmoozefest is by invitation. Donald Trump, Bill Clinton and OJ Simpson have yet to appear, and Chris Evans won't be appearing again.

A FEW USEFUL RANTS

Golfers are inveterate ranters, and bluffers must be no exception. The safest approach is to fulminate on how the modern game is going to hell in a handcart.

Lose no opportunity to complain about slow play, five-hour rounds and four-ball golf (*see* page 59). Lament the decline of the sociable foursome and a creative approach to golf. Impress your companions by suggesting a three-ball sixsome. Inviting them to find a space in the diary for a longest drive competition on the roof of The Savoy, or a match from Oxford to Cambridge, without using a driver or satellite navigation, will have the desired effect. Deplore the golf buggy, and complain about being forced to use one on courses (mostly foreign) with steep hills between holes.

Major championships (*see* 'The Majors and Greats', page 93) merit a prolonged whinge: an endurance test for players and spectators alike, with none of the cut and thrust of matchplay. The Halford Hewitt, now there's a golf tournament, and The Amateur Championship too, plus The President's Putter at Rye, where every January a few Oxbridge diehards shiver in a convincing simulation of golf in Scotland. If you are going to claim to have been there with them, be prepared to answer supplementary questions.

THE WRONG SORT

Like everything else, golf has been a victim of the democratic process. A certain standard of civilised behaviour was for many years maintained by the long-established British club system: you couldn't play unless you belonged to a club, and you couldn't join a club unless you could play.

These days – your rant might continue – any Tom, Darren or Rory can play golf, and does, on municipal or 'pay-and-play' golf courses that admit anyone with a few clubs and a credit card. The rot set in, you will argue, when golf left our shores for America, France and other egalitarian nations. Of course, it is not the new golfer's fault. With no solid grounding in the game, he can hardly be expected to understand the subtleties of etiquette. He turns up at any golf club he chooses, often with disreputable companions, and expects to be allowed to play. Golf clubs can request sight of a handicap certificate, but plausible strictly Internet handicaps are not hard to come by and money talks. Rare is the club whose members would applaud a club secretary/general manager for turning away a green-fee-paying, handicap-certificate-holding, bar-and-restaurant-patronising visitor (*see* 'The Golf Society', page 65).

THE LADIES' GAME

No chapter about the joys of a good golf rant would be complete without mentioning the other half. Male bluffers must take the view that men and women should enjoy equal rights of access and priority on the course and in the clubhouse. This might raise a few beetling eyebrows, but you can redeem yourself by suggesting that ladies might not feel comfortable in the snooker room.

Ladies play a different game, with different clubs, on different days. Many of them do it very well indeed, and are happy in their game. Others hatch the idea that they would like to show men how to do it, because that's the sort of women they are. Many men resist, for the same reason. That's when ranters (predominantly of the male sex) come to the fore.

It all came to a head in 2003 when professional golfer Annika Sörenstam decided to enter a championship on the men's PGA tour on the grounds that it was an 'open' event; she was an open-minded Swedish person and bored of winning everything on the women's tour. Some of the men were furious; others looked on with interest, and expressed polite disappointment when the brave Swede missed the cut. Hawaiian-born Michelle Wie has also assiduously taken on men in successive tournaments, without notable success.

These are noble attempts to liven the game up a bit, but ladies' golf has never quite recaptured the élan and sheer pizzazz it had when Gloria Minoprio reigned supreme. This stylish player, of uncertain provenance and no known handicap, successfully entered the 1933

English Ladies' Open, and on the first day stepped out of a white chauffeured Bentley two minutes before her tee time, in trousers - never before seen on a lady competitor. Minoprio carried a single club in her own image – 'a long-shafted iron with a straight face' – played in complete silence, and lost five and three.

By bluffing her way to the highest level of championship golf, Minoprio is the patroness of our cause, the *ne plus ultra* of bluffing in golf and indeed all sport.

THE MAJORS AND GREATS

Golf goes viral or at least mildly contagious four times a year, when a Major Championship is under way. Inside the clubhouse, golfers stop talking about their own ups and downs for a few days, and move on to the subject of Lee Westwood's putting and commentator Peter Alliss's latest hilarious *bon mot*.

Outside, in the real world, bluffers can show off their knowledge of golf without fear of being considered a bore. Ian Poulter's trousers and Darren Clarke's tobacco take on new fascination as talking points at fashionable social events. Peter Alliss's latest outrageous politically incorrect ejaculation is always a hot topic.

The Majors are the four championships universally acknowledged to be more important than all the others that go on all over the world week after week; year in, year out. Instead of playing in separate tournaments in order to win more often and maximise their income, all the best players come together for the Majors, and Major wins measure the lasting stature of a golfer, much to the annoyance of Colin Montgomerie who won everything else but for some reason never quite closed the deal at a Major. Golf being what it is, a game of chance, this is just bad luck, but bluffers and journalists enjoy picking through the deep character flaws revealed by anything less than victory. The Majors are all held in America or Great Britain, the ratio of 3 to 1 in favour of America symbolising the special relationship.

The Majors all take the same rather dull form: 72 holes of grindingly slow strokeplay, over four days from Thursday to Sunday. At the half-way stage, competitors who are too far off the lead to have any hope of winning are allowed to give up and enjoy their weekend by a process known as 'The Cut', leaving the rest to struggle on until the marathon finishes on Sunday evening.

Extra holes must be played in the event of a tie, arrangements for the 'play-off' varying from one Major to another. This might sound the most exciting possible outcome, but in fact nobody likes a play-off, which mucks up TV schedules, wrecks budgets and ruins commentators' travel arrangements. The player who takes the blame for the play-off attracts harsh criticism for fluking or choking.

Spare a thought for the unfortunate Stewart Cink who ruined history by beating good old Tom Watson, 59, in a play-off for the 2009 Open. In victory Cink found himself without a friend in the world or even a journalist to be interviewed by.

THE MASTERS

Spring is in the air – in Georgia it is, anyway - when the sporting year kicks off in early April for the first Major,

The Masters, which is unique in being the only Major not to have been nearly won by Colin Montgomerie. It is also the only Major that always happens in the same place: Augusta, a country club for rich conservatives near Atlanta, when the azaleas are out. This makes great television and the best possible publicity for a club which has not the slightest intention of admitting visitors.

'Look,' Warren Buffett and his fellow members seem to be saying to hapless outsiders, 'and see how beautiful our club is. Wouldn't you just love to come and play a round of golf here? No you can't.' For all they know, we might be black or gay or female or in favour of gun control.

The Masters was co-founded in 1934 by leading amateur golfer Bobby Jones and Wall Street financier Clifford Roberts, who set the tone by remarking 'as long as I'm alive, golfers will be white, and caddies will be black'.

Never let it be said that Augusta fails to move with the times. Clifford Roberts opened the door to reform by blowing his brains out in 1977, and Augusta cleverly elected a black member, TV mogul Ron Townsend, before Vijay Singh and Tiger Woods came along to claim honorary membership by winning the Masters.

In 2012 Augusta heard the stentorian voice of women's journalism and admitted two lady members of proven conservative credentials. By virtue of gender and skin colour, Condoleezza Rice was a double-headed token, a win-win for Augusta. Now that golf's leading male-only clubs in Scotland, the R&A and Muirfield, have followed Augusta's lead by voting to admit women, the St Regulus Ladies' Golf Club in St Andrews is one of the last bastions of gender inequality in golf.

Bluffers can score points by showing knowledge of Augusta's annual Champions Dinner, where the champion chooses the menu. Play the Champions Dinner game with your friends and fellow bluffers, by matching the menu choices to the golfer.

A Leek soup; B my mom's confetti cake and vanilla ice cream; C caribou; D cheeseburger and strawberry milkshake; E Wiener schnitzel; F haggis. G fish & chips and The Daily Mirror

1 Tiger Woods; 2 Bernhard Langer; 3 Bubba Watson; 4 Sandy Lyle; 5 Nick Faldo; 6 Mike Weir (clue: he's from Canada); 7 Ian Woosnam

(Answers: A7; B3; C6; D1; E2; F4; G5)

There have been many fine shots played at the Masters, but none to eclipse Gene Sarazen's albatross in 1935 – a 4-wood from 235 yards. This masterfluke forced a 36-hole play-off the next day, and if anything like it ever happened again, the commentary team would want to know why.

The most exciting bit of the Masters is Amen Corner, the short 12th, a lake hole where Tom Weiskopf, mistakenly under the impression that he was auditioning for the movie Tin Cup, reduced his caddie's load and raised the water level in running up a 13. There but for the grace .... Amen.

When the Masters finally ends, the old champion invests the new champion with a dark green member's jacket. Bluffers may be asked to explain how Augusta knows what size to make the jacket when a big fat golfer is coming up the last hole tied for the lead with a pipsqueak of Gary Player dimensions. Answer: Augusta has 300 members, and there is bound to be one whose jacket fits.

THE OPEN CHAMPIONSHIP

The other major Major is The Open which takes place in July, at the height of the British summer, and should never be referred to as the British Open, although foreigners always call it that. A rota of famous links courses takes The Open to beauty spots around the British coast from Blackpool to Dungeness. Wales is excluded but the R&A agreed to let Northern Ireland back on to The Open rota in exchange for a promise to improve the hotels, food, roads, telecommunications and weather; and support Theresa May's minority government. The Open returns frequently to the Old Course at St Andrews on the grounds that it is after all the Home of Golf and commentators can use their scripts from last time.

As golf fever grips the nation over the weekend, bluffers should be ready to pronounce on whether the links game is fair, with its invisible bunkers in the middle of the fairway and humps and hollows that send perfectly good shots careering out of bounds. The best line on this is that golf is not a fair game, and professionals – even American ones - ought to have worked that out by now.

Are the old-fashioned links courses tough enough and long enough for the modern player with a modern driver in hand? Well, over four days of the British summer, at least two days of high wind and rain can be expected, turning a piffling course into the most extreme test of character and clothing technology.

At Open Championship time, bluffers cherish the memory of heroic failures such as Leo Diegel (see page 37), who managed to miss the ball when he had a tiny putt to tie in 1933; Ian Baker Finch who in defence of his title began by losing his hat and driving a ball out of bounds; and the supreme collapsee Jean van de Velde, who looked a cert for The Open at Carnoustie in 1999 but blew it at the last hole in the most cavalier fashion, hitting his ball into the grandstand and then a stream, where he removed his socks in flagrant defiance of the dress code.

Only he didn't quite blow it. Peter Alliss's mounting tide of fury as it became clear that a play-off was likely, delaying his transfer to the 19th hole by more than an hour, was a career highlight. At least Adam Scott had the decency to collapse properly in 2012, managing to lose without a play-off.

On a positive note, Jordan Spieth's exciting charge to victory at Birkdale in 2017 had spectators on the edge of their seats for every second of the 20 minutes it took Spieth to play his second shot at the 13th.

MINOR MAJORS

Either side of The Open come the US Open (June) and the US PGA (August). Bluffers should be aware of these two minor Majors, especially if a British or European golfer is in contention for victory, but any attempt to explain or claim to understand the differences between them goes beyond bluff. Some courses have hosted both the US Open and the PGA, so there can't be all that much difference, can there?

If pressed on this point, mention amateur golfers, who are not allowed at the PGA but brighten up the other three Majors by smiling a lot and reminding us that golf is great fun when no money is involved. There is always one amateur who plays a couple of good rounds and can be pressurised by the media in to turning professional far too soon. Here cite the example of Justin Rose who nearly won The Open as an amateur, took many years to win his first golf game as a professional and looked in contention for a place in history as another Best Golfer Never to Win a Major, until something went wrong.

The attractive parallel topic of the Worst Golfers to Win a Major is for advanced bluffers only, and should be reserved for very wet days in the clubhouse. Stewart Cink is usually on the list. Not that there is much wrong with his swing. Everyone hates him for beating nice Mr Watson, that's all.

OLYMPIC GOLF

Golf watchers and golfers themselves were uncertain about the best line to take when golf made its debut as an Olympic sport at Rio in 2016. Many top players decided to give the Games a miss, and it goes without saying that this had nothing to do with money. It was important to show solidarity with the Northern Irish contingent who found it hard to know which country to represent, and with the tabloid press in a frenzy about the Zika virus, the golfers had their families to consider. In retrospect it became blindingly obvious that those who stayed away had taken the wrong decision.

This had nothing to do with Justin Rose winning gold for Great Britain, of course. In a young country where golf's growth potential is unlimited – it's almost unheard of – Olympic golf was a great boost for the game.

THE RYDER CUP

This biennial competition is the best school of tactical golf: a matchplay team event which pits Europe against the USA, the original format (Britain against the USA) having proved unfairly one-sided. Honest patriotic fervour can be relied on to spill over into ugly xenophobia and bitter argument after a couple of matches, with much waving of flags, cheering at lost balls and missed putts, mid-swing coughing, camera-shutter-clicking and all the rest of it, for real. Golf's veneer of gentility peels back to reveal a nasty game, and a few not altogether nice people.

'You can have the hole and the goddamn cup,' Ken Still snarled at Bernard Gallacher at the end of a particularly bad-tempered match, but that was the exception. As a rule, the Americans are much better losers than the Europeans, who are still muttering about Kiawah Island (golfers dressed aggressively in what looked like Shock and Awe combat uniforms) and the Brookline affair in 1999, when a spectator moved while a European golfer was standing over his putt. 'Outrageous!' fumed the

European vice-captain Sam Torrance. The Americans insisted their man in the crowd only oscillated. At the closing press conference, all habitually agree that golf itself has been the winner, and it takes only a couple of years for the special relationship to recover, before the whole thing happens again.

At the time of writing the detail of Britain's future relationship with Europe has yet to be thrashed out. Golfers voted for Brexit in 2016, without thinking through its implications for the Ryder Cup, where Team Europe flies the EU flag. A transitional period while a new flag is designed is one possible way forward, but the safest bet is to steer clear of the whole subject. Europe's 2016 Ryder Cup captain Darren Clarke's remark that "the UK is always going to be part of the European continent" was not exactly conclusive.

GOLFING GREATS

Who was the greatest? In order to join in the conversation on a wet day in the clubhouse, you'll need a few key facts at your fingertips.

League A

Hagen, Walter Sharp dresser, sharp talker, successful bluffer: 'you're only here for a short visit, so be sure to smell the flowers along the way.'

Jones, Bobby Nice American amateur. 'You might as well praise a man for not robbing a bank' (after calling a penalty on himself).

Morris, (various), mostly called *Tom*. Mostly related.

Hogan, Ben Famous for 'that' swing.

Vardon, Harry Elegant swinger from Jersey, six times winner of The Open.

Palmer, Arnold Just what the dull sport of golf needed, before it needed Seve Ballesteros.

Ballesteros, Seve A legend in your own lifetime but alas no longer his. Golf as theatre. Mention the car park shot at Lytham (The Open, 1979). Don't mention the 'early walking' (starting to walk away from the tee while the opponent is in mid-backswing).

Woods, Tiger Those whom the gods wish to punish... classical tragedy, not yet played out.

Nicklaus, Jack The Golden Bear, let down by squeaky voice. Luckily, Nicklaus's record speaks for itself.

Norman, Greg The Great White Shirt. Rugged clothing entrepreneur easily wound up at press conferences by mentioning 'bottling it' at Augusta, and running off with his best friend's wife (Chris Evert).

Faldo, Nick 'All my wives misunderstand me' (and they're not the only ones).

Watson, Tom Might have won The Open at the age of 59,

but it was just too much to hope for. Don't forget the unforgettable 'duel in the sun' with Jack Nicklaus (Turnberry, 1977) in the best weather that Scotland can remember.

League B

Jacklin, Tony The best thing to come out of Potters Bar since the Great North Road.

Player, Gary You can't forget Player, though you might like to. He keeps popping up and giving interviews to remind us how good he is/was.

Woosnam, Ian A little woozy. Welsh. Almost certainly the shortest golfer ever to win the Masters.

Lyle, Sandy Once a great ball striker, always a great ball striker. Once a Masters champion, always entitled to have a go.

De Vicenzo, Roberto Argentinian gentleman. 'What a stupid I am!' (after signing his card for one shot too many).

Langer, Bernhard Never up, never in. Easily done. We've all missed shorter putts than that. (Not with the Ryder Cup at stake, however.)

Daly, John Big man, big swing, small problem (*see* 'Golf and Addiction'). Lovely touch for someone so…you know, how should we put it, big.

Montgomerie, Colin Bad luck Colin. Cheer up old chap.

Singh, Vijay Never suggest he cheated.

Clarke, Darren Somehow held on at Sandwich. Golf's best-known smoker.

Sörenstam, Annika Forced her way on to the men's tour to prove golf has embraced gender equality. Results inconclusive.

Davies, Laura Dame Laura, and don't you forget it.

Trevino, Lee Comedy Tex-Mex. Never took a lesson, never needed one (at gamesmanship anyway).

Mickelson, Phil Smiling left-hander, until America lost the 2014 Ryder Cup. Then the smile faded and the truth came out.

McIlroy, Rory Brilliant Irish golfer with a great future, now possibly behind him.

Spieth, Jordan All over the place off the tee, deadly from 30 feet. Faux humility undermined by use of Royal We.

Johnson, Dustin Distance, accuracy, substance issues. DJ has it all.

Garcia, Sergio The Best Golfer Not To Win A Major, no longer. At last.

Reed, Patrick Brash American who endeared himself to millions and ensured immortality by yelling 'you f*****' faggot' after three-putting.

PRESIDENTIAL GOLF

Many golfers have enjoyed success in public life, climbing the greasy pole by means of competitive strategies learned on the golf course. You might think that world leaders would be too busy to fit in much golf, but you would be wrong. Delegation, after all, is the secret of leadership.

While Vladimir Putin promotes a half-naked image of himself on horseback, American presidents hold press conferences at golf clubs to boast about how many rounds they have played since inauguration (not always counting every shot along the way). Way out in front is Eisenhower (800+ rounds), who played so much golf that Vice President Nixon felt obliged to take up the game himself. At 400 rounds each, Clinton and Obama tried hard but were no match for Ike; Ford, Reagan and both Bushes also played. Having been critical of Eisenhower's golf, JFK kept quiet about his own love of the game until golf proved to be useful cover for other activities best kept from the wife.

Kennedy was a fine college player, but Donald Trump's harshest critics concede that the 45th president is the best golfer to have made it to the Oval Office, if not the best at adding up. They have even suggested that a man who so obviously feels more at home on the golf course than in the White House might consider playing more often, and spend less time interfering in politics.

Although British prime ministers enjoy free golf at Ellesborough Golf Club near Chequers, according to the terms of a leasehold deal negotiated by Lloyd George, few recent leaders have seen golf as a vote winner south of the border, especially if you play in jeans, as David Cameron did at St Enodoc. If that was a faux pas, with hindsight Cameron may reflect that accepting a golf challenge from Barack Obama in April 2016 – the president's 286th game in office - was a more serious blunder. Allowing himself to be photographed holding the putter upside down was bad for the PM's image, and losing the match further damaged his cause in the EU Referendum. Cameron's departure from office soon followed.

Other role models include King Hassan II of Morocco, who played every day, followed by a queue of ministers bearing important documents such as execution orders for dissidents, to be signed between green and tee. Such was the monarch's dedication to the game, he installed a floodlit course inside the palace walls for night-time golf during Ramadan.

Bluffers can reassure anxious club members that Fidel Castro and Che Guevara – always in breach of the dress code - were not in fact golfers, they merely posed with clubs for a photoshoot before razing Havana Country Club. It would be bad form to spoil the story of Dear Leader Kim Jong-il's famous 18-hole score of 34 shots, including five holes in one, by mentioning the oriental caddie's custom of marking the scorecard not with the number of shots taken at each hole, but the number of shots above par.

Moving off with screams of jubilant celebration before the opponent has putted is frightfully inconsiderate. Any Ryder Cup match will show you exactly how to do this.

There's no point in pretending that you know everything about golf – nobody does – but if you've got this far and absorbed at least a modicum of the information and advice contained within these pages, then you will almost certainly know more than 99% of the rest of the human race about what golf is, why it plays such a central role in many people's lives, why it can drive you mad, and how you can pretend to be better at it than you are.

What you now do with this information is up to you, but here's a suggestion: be confident about your new-found knowledge, see how far it takes you, but above all have fun using it. You are now a bona fide expert in the art of bluffing about the world's most frustrating game. Just don't ever expect to master it.

GLOSSARY

Address
1. Links View, Westward Ho! isn't bad.
2. The beginning of the shot. Wiggling the head to and fro is fine; you can shift your feet, twitch your bottom, clench and unclench your right hand, and waggle the club all you like. But once you have touched the ground with the club head, you are deemed to have addressed the ball. Whatever you do next will count as a shot, so you may as well hit the thing.

Air shot A miss. Also practice shot (*see* 'Handicaps (and Gamesmanship)', page 39).

Albatross Large bird, rarely seen. Also a score of three under par on an individual hole. It's never going to happen so don't worry about it. Americans, showing a poor understanding of ornithology and maths, call it a double eagle.

Anchoring Steadying the putter against a body part

less shaky than your hands; illegal (from 2016) unless you did it by mistake (from 2019).

As it lies Where the ball comes to rest: usually in a small hole, burrow or divot, or behind a tree, wall or other obstruction. In their fairness, the Rules of Golf usually require a ball to be played as it lies, but winter rules may help by allowing the ball to be 'cleaned' (moved).

As we lie Golfers say this to one another as a reminder that at this stage of the hole, their contest could not be more finely balanced. Typically the player whose ball sits a couple of inches from the hole after two shots says to his opponent, when the latter's second lands in a bunker: 'As we lie?'

Backspin Spin is the professional's secret. By applying it, he can land the ball anywhere on the green, and it will stay there. The amateur has a target landing strip of about three yards at the front of the green – any shorter and he is in the sand, or water; any longer, and he rolls over the back. Ask a pro to teach you how to spin the ball, and he will laugh, patting you on the shoulder patronisingly.

Bad lie You soon get used to this in golf. Typical examples are: 'I drove the ball 260 yards,' 'What a shame one of us had to lose,' and 'I don't care how badly I play, it's just great to be here.'

Baffy Ancient name for a 4-wood. The most experienced caddie can be put in his place by a request for a baffy.

Birdie One shot under par. Rare, but worth mentioning. Golfers go on about it for ages.

Bisque An extra stroke, generously donated over and above the handicap allowance, and used as a desperate measure by golfers who are in the soup. 'At this point, we have to use our bisque.'

Brassie Archaic name for a 2-wood with a brass sole. Careful how you say that to the club captain.

Bunker A deep hole full of sand with an overhanging cliff face on the side nearest the green. Americans call bunkers 'traps', can't imagine why.

Caddie Now rare. Using a caddie marks you out as a confident golfer who plays well enough not to be put off by bad advice and a scornful attitude.

Cleek
1. An old iron club corresponding to the modern 1- or 2-iron.
2. The committee (if you meant clique).

Divot A lump of fairway that is a bad thing if it travels farther than the ball, but a good thing if your opponent's ball comes to rest in one.

Dog-leg A hole which bends sharply to the right or left and offers players the choice of cutting the corner or playing safe. So long as you don't declare your intention in advance, any kind of shot can be presented as deliberate.

Draw
1. A shot that moves out to the right and then in again (reverse the instructions if you're left-handed). All golfers aspire to this 'shape', but its superiority to the straight hit has yet to be conclusively demonstrated, unless there is a tree in the way.
2. A hook.

Driver A straight-faced wooden club. The idea is to hit the ball a long way, but this may not be an advantage if it goes in the wrong direction. As a rule of thumb, when tempted to use the driver, don't.

Eagle Two shots under par. It's not going to happen.

Fade
1. The opposite of a draw, and much less fashionable.
2. A slice.

Fairway The narrowest part of the golf course, and the most exposed. It is hard to conceal your actions from public view or find anything to blame for a bad shot. Luckily the grass is kept very short and the ball usually rolls off the fairway into the rough, where excuses abound.

Fluff Easily removed from the green, but make sure you don't press the grass (two stroke penalty).

Foozle A duff, fluff, mishit, pear-shaped, complete Horlicks. Popular with polite Americans, it belongs to another age and should be allowed to rest in peace.

Fore 'Watch out!' Also: 'Get a move on you old fool!'

Free drop Rarely offered to an opponent before he has conceded the hole. The subtext is: 'I may call in the favour later.'

Gimme A short putt you think you may well miss and you invite your opponent to concede. If he is more than four up, he might.

Good (also okay, right, all right, have, give) Word, if uttered on green, likely to be seized on by your opponent as evidence that a putt has been conceded.

Green An area of smooth grass with a hole in the bumpy bit.

Green fee The cost of a round of golf: incalculable, financially and emotionally.

Ground Under Repair Newly dug graves, archaeological zones and other parts of the course where golfers have had a spot of bother.

Hazard The last place you want to be on a golf course; more or less anywhere in an arc of 180 degrees of a golfer preparing to hit a ball. Or even 360 degrees if it hits his foot.

Hickory. Vintage wooden-shafted club designed to separate golfers from bluffers. You have been warned.

Hole out Hit the ball into the hole. This is the general idea of golf, but many players go complete rounds without achieving it.

Honesty box For green fees; always empty.

Honour. The winner of the last hole has the 'honour' of playing first. 'Your honour, your honour' is a golf joke that never wears thin.

Hook An indecisive shot that starts off on the right and ends up miles to the left, usually lost, and sometimes known as a Stansgate (aka Tony Benn, the former viscount of the same name). When played by a left-hander, the hook travels from left to the extreme right and may be called a Blair.

Iron Metal rarely used in golf, although when clubs were made entirely of wood, those that were not woods (or putters) had iron heads.

Jigger
1. An inn in St Andrews; a bit touristy and overpriced these days.
2. (Obsolete) narrow-bladed club used for short shots to the green.

Lay up Tactical golf shot to save going through the back of the green. If your approach shot from 100 yards out lands well short, you laid up.

Lie
1. Your game, as told to friends and family.
2. Ground condition where the ball lies, usually bad. Improving the lie is prohibited, but one way to get away with it is to pick the ball up 'to check that it's mine'.

Lost ball A ball should be declared lost if not found in five minutes (or three, depending on when you're reading). After four minutes and 50 seconds of searching, wave the game behind through and you may be able to look for another five minutes. If you still can't find it, try looking in your trouser leg or pocket. It might just have got caught in there.

Mashie All-purpose iron club – 5-iron, roughly – with many variations. Mashie niblick, spade mashie, fork mashie, mashie spoon, mish mashie, steam iron, any old iron.

Medal A monthly golf competition won by annoyingly consistent people. Every hole must be completed, and every shot counts. This may be fair, but it's no fun.

Niblick Yet another old iron club with a sloping face, quite like a 9-iron but much more evocative.

Par The score you ought to make if you were any good.

Play through When looking for a ball, resting or playing with someone who needs 14 practice strokes for every shot, etiquette requires you to invite the game behind to overtake. Those playing through will say 'thanks very much' before making a complete hash of their shots, with lost balls in much the same location as yours. It is then hard to know how to proceed, but there may be yet another game coming up behind that can be waved through, ultimately leading to total paralysis on the course.

Provisional It does no harm to say 'provisional' before every shot, to indicate that you are probably going to lose the ball but, just in case, here goes.

Putt The only part of the game that matters. Golf has been described as a game of 'ifs and putts'. About its vital importance in the game you will say: 'Drive for show, putt for dough.'

Rake A useful tool for stopping your ball before it rolls in to the bunker. Send the caddie forward to arrange the rakes before you drive.

Ray, Ted British golfer (1877-1943). When asked for advice on how to hit the ball farther, he replied: 'Hit it harder.'

Rescue club A broad-headed club – probably a wood, but it's hard to tell these days – designed to get a ball out of a bad lie. The most effective design has four fingers and a thumb.

R&A An exclusive golf club in St Andrews with no course of its own. Confused? Wait until you try reading the Rules of Golf.

Scramble, or Texas Scramble A tedious team game devised by good golfers and patronisingly described by them as 'great fun'. The rules allow bad players to take part but not count or influence the outcome.

Scratch A golfer whose handicap is zero (i.e., someone who does not need to bluff).

Shank A dreadful mishap. No one knows what causes it, but the symptoms are familiar to all. When it happens, blame the 'hosel': you may need the pro to 'realign' it.

Slice See 'Fade.'

Spoon Now called a 3-wood. Golfers are fond of exchanging spoonerisms such as 'you chucking feat'.

Stableford A friendly strokeplay scoring system popular among bad golfers. You can make a complete hash of a hole, or take a few holes off, and still win.

Stroke Index An extremely complicated mechanism for working out when to give your opponent, who has a higher handicap than you, an extra stroke (or two).

Stymie Blocking manoeuvre. The stymie is a rare example of a golfing term that has completed the journey into everyday life, and left golf behind. The tactic of using your ball to block your opponent's route to the hole, as in a snooker, was removed from golf in 1952, and as a result few golfers now bother to master the art of the swerved putt.

Tee
1. Untidy area littered with bits of coloured plastic, sweet wrappers and vulgar advertising notices at the beginning of each hole.
2. Small plastic or broken wooden peg used to make holes in trouser pockets, fill ashtrays in bedrooms, break washing machines and record the score when you've lost all your pencils. The ball may be placed on a tee at the beginning of each hole. That's all the help you are going to get, so you might as well use it.

Twitch Putter's disease best cured by regular infusions of alcohol.

Twosome A small, intimate dinner party, not to be confused with competitive golf between two players, usually described as a 'game of golf' or 'match'.

Wedge A club with a steeply sloping face invented by the champion show-off Gene Sarazen and designed for flashy trick shots that send the ball high in the air without forward progress.

Whiff An air shot in America. Many golfers take

umbrage at the suggestion of a whiff, and it is easy to see why.

Winter rules The golf club is a relaxed place during the winter months. Members are allowed to wipe the mud off their ball before hitting it. And then replace it in a more advantageous lie.

Woods
1. Long-haul clubs made of graphite, Kevlar, carbon fibre, steel or almost anything except wood.
2. Tigerish golfer who scored too much, too often and in all the wrong places, and had to take a break and seek therapy after he drove his car into a tree.

A BIT MORE BLUFFING...

Available from all good bookshops

bluffers.com